Southern Mountain Guitar

By Wayne Erbsen

Southern Mountain Guitar is just one in an exciting series of 5 books. Included in this series are *Southern Mountain Banjo, Southern Mountain Dulcimer, Southern Mountain Fiddle,* and *Southern Mountain Mandolin.* Each book features vintage photos, history, instruction and music designed to accompany each instrument. A great way to learn and play Southern Mountain music!

A recording of the music in this book is now available. The publisher strongly recommends the use of this recording along with the text to insure accuracy of interpretation and ease in learning.

Contents

Alphabetical List of Tunes

How To Use This Book

Southern Mountain Guitar is based on the sixteen tunes found on the recording *Southern Mountain Classics*. It is written for the beginner, intermediate and advanced guitar player and is designed to be used with this recording. Please keep in mind that none of the arrangements in the book are exact transcriptions of the music on the recording. Most of the recorded tunes, in fact, don't even have lead guitar on them. Nonetheless, all of the tunes on the recording are included in the book. Even before you spread the book out in front of you, it is suggested you sit back and listen to the recording.

The book is broken down in two parts.

PART I BACKGROUND: Includes an introduction to Southern mountain music.

PART II THE TUNES: The 16 tunes on *Southern Mountain Classics* are written out in musical notation and guitar tablature. For each tune there is a song history and two versions of each tune labeled Version I or Version II, depending on the level of difficulty. Also provided for each tune is the chord structure to help you play rhythm guitar along with the recording.

Order of the tunes to play: The tunes in the book are arranged in *alphabetical order,* to make finding them easier.

As you listen to the recording, some tunes will be familiar to you while others may not. The first tunes you should begin to play are the ones that you have heard before or that seem easiest to you.

Tip: Practice singing or humming along with the recording until you get the tunes in your head. Once you have a firm grip on the melody of a particular tune it will be much easier to read the notes found in this book. In fact, on some of the tunes you may even want to try picking out the tunes off the recording *without* using the book. When you get stumped, you can then refer to the music or tablature.

Good Luck, and Keep Pickin',

Wayne Erbsen

Wayne Erbsen

Southern Mountain Music

Southern mountain music is like a precious patchwork that was carefully sewn stitch by stitch over the years. This quilt was like no other ever sewn; the rugged terrain of the mountains saw to that. Mountains like the Appalachians, the Alleghenies and the Blue Ridge kept communities cut off from the outside world. Though this isolation was never complete, it did tend to slow down the pace of change. For mountain people, the old ways were preferred over the "new fangled." So it was that the old music, the old dances, and the old stories from England, Ireland, and Scotland were held on to long after they were abandoned by communities more in touch with the changes that were taking place all over America.

Ballads:

When the English and Scotch-Irish settled in the Southern Mountains, the ballads were among the few precious keepsakes they were able to carry with them. When Englishman Cecil Sharp came to the mountains around 1916, he was astonished to find many of the old English ballads and songs were better preserved in America than in the British Isles themselves. Had he collected fiddle tunes, hymns and jack tales, he would have found the same thing to be true. What he did find was that Southern mountain people, especially the women, had preserved the old ballads almost intact. The ballads were still sung unaccompanied in solo voice, and often lasted for five minutes or more. He found the ballads were sung while doing housework or for family entertainment in the evening. One woman with nine children reportedly sang constantly while doing her chores so her children would always know where to find her. Eventually many of the ballads were shortened and straightened out to accommodate the accompaniment of stringed instruments like banjos, guitars and dulcimers. Many of the words and phrases of the ballads and even the twists and turns of the melodies showed up in newly composed songs and fiddle tunes.

Photo reproduced from the collections of the Library of Congress.

The Fiddle:

 The fiddle was the backbone of old-time dance music. Lightweight and easy to carry, it was the most transportable of all the old-time instruments, with the exception of the voice. Many early immigrants from the British Isles thus carried fiddles with them aboard the sailing ships that docked in the New World. Equally important as the instruments themselves was the vast store of fiddle tunes that these early settlers carried with them to America. These melodies were the seeds out of which grew old-time music. Though English settlers were numerically superior to other immigrants from the British Isles, their impact was primarily in the songs and ballads they brought with them. The Irish and Scottish people seem to have contributed the most to what became the Southern mountain fiddling tradition. In England there was a popular expression: "If you can't sing, then play a tune." In Ireland and Scotland the reverse was true: "If you can't play a tune then sing."

The fiddle proved to be among the most versatile instruments. In early mountain settlements it alone held sway for the many community dances that were held. These dances were often the most popular social gatherings in rural America. Any excuse to hold a dance was fair game. Dances were held to celebrate a barn-raising, corn shucking, molasses stir-off, apple-butter boiling, flax-pulling, you name it. The popularity of these early dances gave an important function to the fiddle, which provided the music. A community that could boast an ace fiddler or two at a square dance was the envy of all. In some communities where homemade liquor ran free and law enforcement was lax, community dances sometimes provided an opportunity for long-held feuds to flair up. Occasionally shots rang out over the sound of fiddles, banjos, and dancing feet. The unfortunate association of violence and rowdy behavior with community dances led in some areas to their eventual decline. In their place, more tightly controlled square dance clubs have remained popular to this day. Unfortunately, in later years many clogging teams and square dance groups came to rely on recorded dance music rather than on the real thing.

Besides playing for square dances, fiddlers also performed waltzes, shottishes, quadrilles, highland flings, quicksteps, jigs and hornpipes. Eventually, most of these dances lost favor and went out of style in many Southern mountain communities. Only the square dance, the Virginia Reel and the waltz remained popular. Unfortunately, when the earlier dances lost favor, so too did the tunes and rhythms that once accompanied them. Gone from the repertoire of most Southern fiddlers were the jigs, the quadrilles, the shottishes and the highland fings. These tunes were either forgotten or were played as reels. Even hornpipes like "Fisher's Hornpipe," which remained in the repertoire of many mountain fiddlers, were played as a reel.

Although the fiddle was among the most beloved and respected of all musical instruments, it was also one of the most despised. To some religious fundamentalists, the fiddle was the "instrument of the devil" and playing the fiddle was scornfully referred to as doing "the devil's handiwork." Fiddle tunes such as "The Devil's Dream" and "Devil in the Strawstack" and folk expressions like "Thick as fiddlers in Hell" did not help to diminish this unsavory reputation. Even the practice of keeping a rattlesnake rattle inside the fiddle as a good omen was looked on suspiciously.

The Dulcimer:

The music of the fiddle and the singing of the English ballads were soon joined in the Southern mountains by the dulcimer. Early dulcimers evolved in the late eighteenth and early nineteenth centuries from a German instrument called a scheitholt. These instruments often had three or four strings and were narrow in width with long, straight sides. The frets were embedded directly into the top of the instrument. In the mountains, the scheitholt was eventually given the name dulcimer, from the earlier hammered dulcimer, which was frequently mentioned in the Bible. The word dulcimer comes from the Greek "dulce," or sweet, and the Latin word "melos," or song.

Southern mountain dulcimer makers experimented wildly in an effort to make the instrument more playable. A separate raised fretboard was added in the middle of the instrument which was usually hollowed out to allow the instrument more resonance. The instrument was widened and given curved sides and often a scrolled peghead like the fiddle. Various string combinations were experimented with and even to this day it is common for dulcimers to have anywhere from three to eight strings. Sometimes strings are found grouped in pairs and sometimes not. The string pattern that seems to be the most common in modern dulcimers is for the melody strings to be in pairs and the two other strings to be spaced evenly.

Among the things that make the dulcimer unique is the spacing of the frets. Unlike the guitar or the banjo which were fretted chromatically, the frets on the dulcimer are fretted diatonically. This means that a dulcimer fretboard contains wide fret spaces which represent the whole tones and narrower spaces which are the half tones. The dulcimer fretboard is thus similar to the white keys of the piano, making it relatively easy to coax a tune out of the instrument.

Dulcimers were commonly played with the fingers, but various "picks" have been utilized including turkey quills, willow switches, and oak splints. On rare occasions dulcimers have even been bowed. The left hand is used for noting the strings, but occasionally dulcimer players have used a wooden "noter" to fret the strings.

The dulcimer became popular in the backwoods of the Southern mountains. It was considered to be a safe and proper instrument by those God-fearing people who felt the fiddle to be a rakish instrument played only for rowdy dances. The dulcimer was perfect for accompanying the old songs and hymns.

Among the more unusual adaptions of the dulcimer was the addition of a second fretboard with its own set of strings. This instrument was known as a harmonium or courting dulcimer. Courting was facilitated because to play this instrument correctly, a young couple had to sit opposite each other with their knees touching. This shocking activity often led many couples to the gates of matrimony.

Two children taking corn to grist mill for meal. Mt. Pisgah, North Carolina, 1915.
Photo by William Barnhill, courtesy Mars Hill College, Southern Appalachian Photographic Archives.

The Banjo:

Although the banjo may have originated in distant Africa or the Middle East, it was in America that it developed into the instrument we know today. At first slave banjos were made from a gourd with a skin stretched across it. As early as 1678 such an instrument was known as a "banza." Later names included bangil, banjer, banshaw, banjar, banjoe. The banjo remained an instrument of black slaves until the 1830s when Southern white musicians first began playing the banjo. By the early 1840s musicians like Ben Cotton claimed to have learned from black banjo players while working on Mississippi river boats, and Joel Sweeney studied the banjo playing of slaves on his family's plantation in Virginia.

In 1843 there arose a new style of music that would soon take the country by storm. Known as "minstrel music," it began in the unlikely setting of New York City. Daniel D. Emmett, Joel Sweeney, Thomas Rice and others created an appealing stage show that pretended to portray Southern plantation life and music. Sporting names like *The Virginia Minstrels,* and *The Ethiopian Serenaders,* a typical minstrel show was often a rowdy affair with numerous minstrels suited up in black face and often outlandish costumes playing banjo, fiddle, bones, tambourine, jawbone, and dancing. The show consisted of rousing songs, spirited instrumentals, wild dancing, outrageous stump speeches, earthy jokes, and hilarious skits. The minstrels often had to compete with the audience for attention as minstrel goers tended to be as raucous as the musicians themselves.

The sound and spirit of the minstrel shows captured the attention of the nation in what was described as a "minstrel craze." Minstrel troupes traversed the country from the east coast to the gold fields of California and even performed on stages in the cities of Western Europe.

Rural Southerners, even in remote places, were also caught up in the minstrel craze for better than fifty years. Some minstrels like Joe Sweeney traveled by horse and buggy while others joined lavish minstrel shows aboard steamboats with such names as "Mountain Boy" and "Banjo." Minstrel troupes also performed in concert halls, saloons, traveling circuses, street fairs and anywhere they could draw a crowd. Minstrel shows were especially popular with soldiers during the Civil War. Confederate General Jeb Stuart, in fact, employed banjoist Sam Sweeney, the brother of Joel Sweeney, to keep his troops entertained.

Although the heyday of the minstrel show started to wane by the 1880s, it forever left its stamp on American music. It established the banjo as a popular instrument and gave us many of our most enduring songs including Dan Emmett's "Dixie," "Blue Fly Tail," "Old Dan Tucker" and "Turkey in the Straw," Stephen Foster compositions like "Oh! Susanna," "My Old Kentucky Home," "Old Black Joe," "Swannee River," and James A. Bland's "Oh, Them Golden Slippers" and "Carry Me Back to Old Virginny."

By the 1870s, the banjo had taken a firm root among mountain musicians. Most played in what was sometimes called the clawhammer style learned from watching black musicians or minstrels. This style also went by such names as frailing, rapping, knocking, drop-thumb, whamming, banging and thumb-cocking. Mountain people took to the banjo because it was adaptable to playing the old songs and ballads from long ago, and for playing in a rhythmic manner suitable for a square dance or frolic. The banjo was also easy to play on the new minstrel and Civil War songs and could be used for serenading a sweetheart with a newly composed love ditty. A banjo could easily be built in a home workshop with a groundhog skin stretched across a small wooden hoop. These so-called mountain banjos were a fretless and soft-spoken instrument suitable for playing solo instrumental tunes or for playing simple accompaniment to old-time mountain songs and ballads. Beginning as early as 1831, professional banjo makers like Henry C. Dobson began producing factory-made instruments. However, it was not until about 1880 that banjo manufacturers started adding frets to their instruments. Gradually these fretted factory-made instruments began to compete with the homemade fretless banjos in the mountains.

Around the turn of the century, the banjo experienced a revival in the larger Northern cities. Banjo societies and banjo orchestras became the latest craze and professional banjo builders like S.S. Stewart, and W.A. Cole could hardly keep up with the demand to produce everything from tiny piccolo banjos to gigantic bass-banjos. Rural musicians reaped the benefits of this incredible period of banjo construction. When the fad died out, the used but often magnificent instruments could be bought for a song. Many of these fine instruments ended up in the hands of lucky Southern musicians.

TOP: Left to right:
Joe Maphis and
"Travis Picker"
Merle Travis, 1954.

LEFT: "Scruggs Style Picker"
Earl Scruggs at
Grand Ole' Opry Mike, 1957.

The Guitar:

Guitars were well-known by Colonial times and President John Tyler's wife Julia was even known to have played one in the White House in her "Ethiopian Band," as she called it. However, guitars in early mountain music were scarce. Not until after the turn of the century did guitars become introduced to mountain music. The availability of cheap guitars through mail order catalogs made them available and affordable for the first time. A guitar could be purchased through the Sears & Roebuck catalog for a whopping $2.45 delivered to your door.

The guitar spread like wildfire through the mountains. Perhaps it gained so fast a foothold because mountain people were learning to accept the changes brought on by a growth of towns and cities. Its popularity was also due to the fact that the guitar was a novel instrument that was easy to play and could stand alone, or be used to accompany a fiddle, a banjo or the singing of an old ballad.

With its rapid acceptance by mountain musicians, the guitar made an enormous impact on changing the sound of mountain music. These changes were a result of the fact that the guitar was a chorded instrument. When guitars were added, the music was changed to fit into the three major chords that most major guitarists used for accompaniment. The beautiful modal tunes which were based on gapped or pentatonic scales did not fit well with the guitar, so many of these haunting melodies were put aside in favor of the more cheerful sound of the guitar. The steady squared-off rhythm of the guitar also effected the music. Many of the old ballads and tunes contained extra beats and were "crooked" as the roads that wound around the mountains. When these uneven turns and crooks met up with the guitar, they were straightened out just like the roads eventually were.

As the guitar was accepted into mountain music, various changes to the instrument itself became necessary. The small and delicate "parlor guitars" that were popular a generation before, gave way to larger and more powerful "dreadnought" guitars named after a World War I battleship. At first, guitars provided mere accompaniment to the more flamboyant banjos and fiddles. Gradually, however, guitar techniques developed to a point where a guitar player could go toe to toe and elbow to elbow with the finest fiddler or banjo player. Early recording artists like Riley Puckett, Maybelle Carter, Charlie Monroe, the Delmore Brothers, and later Merle Travis and Doc Watson helped to advance the guitar to a higher level.

The Carter Family.

The Mandolin:

The earliest mandolins were imported to America from Germany and Italy. These often ornate instruments had a flat top and round back and were affectionately referred to as "Tator Bugs" by rural musicians. Instrument makers Lyon and Healey of Chicago produced Washburn mandolins that satisfied the small but growing demand for instruments to accompany the playing and singing of popular tunes of the day.

Starting in the 1870s, it was Orville Gibson working in his shop in Kalamazoo, Michigan who dramatically changed the basic shape and construction of the mandolin. Orville's instruments were the first mandolins whose tops and backs were carved much like the instruments of the violin family. He replaced the round back design of traditional mandolins, which were difficult to play, with a gently curved back similar to a violin. This change alone greatly improved the tone and increased the ease of playing the instrument.

By the turn of the century Orville began having trouble keeping up with the demand for his high quality instruments. In fact, when one store requested terms, costs and shipping dates for five hundred instruments, Orville replied it would take five hundred years to fill the order. Eventually, however, Orville found backers who invested in the Gibson Mandolin-Guitar Manufacturing Co., Limited. Even with the increased size of the operation, Gibson was still able to turn out mandolins which were superior in construction and projected greater volume and tone than anything that had come before.

By 1902, mandolin societies and orchestras became popular and Gibson and other instrument builders like S.S. Stewart and C.F. Martin had a heyday keeping up with the new demand for mandolins, mandolas, mando-cello, and even mando-bases. Audiences flocked to hear the mandolin on concert stage, in vaudeville, and on the new recordings that were coming out.

By about 1920, the heyday of the mandolin orchestra began to wane. Ragtime was the new rage. Interest in the mandolin was transferred to the tenor banjo, which was tuned and played similar to the mandolin, only louder. Mandolin manufacturers responded by producing the mandolin-banjo, which had a mandolin neck on a banjo body. Even this did not stop the steady decline in interest in the mandolin.

Although mandolins were rarely used in early Southern mountain music, they gradually gained in importance at the very time they were losing favor elsewhere. Many of the fine instruments that had formerly been played in mandolin orchestras slowly filtered into the hands of musicians in rural communities where they took their place in string bands alongside the fiddle, banjo and guitar. With these fine instruments at their disposal, mandolins were finally able to compete with the much louder banjos and fiddles. The advent of phonograph records and radios also helped build acceptance of the mandolin in rural areas. With a turn of a knob, a recording engineer could balance the softer tones of the mandolin with the louder volumes of other instruments.

During the 1930s brother duets like the Monroe Brothers, the Bolick Brothers and the Morris Brothers featured the mandolin as a lead instrument and further added to its reputation and popularity among country people. These musicians were especially popular in North Carolina, where they criss-crossed the state performing in school houses, theaters and on the radio. By October of 1939, Bill Monroe had taken his newly-formed band known as The Blue Grass Boys to the stage of the Grand Ole Opry which helped to fuel a revival of the mandolin and to give recognition to the style of music that would soon be known as bluegrass.

Traveling Medicine Shows:

Even before the passing of the minstrel show in the 1890s, popular entertainment was often mixed with a large dose of quackery to produce what was called the traveling medicine show. Such shows actually began in Europe and were found in the American colonies by the early eighteenth century.

The traveling medicine show's methods were quite simple: to attract and hold audiences long enough for a pitchman to convince its members to part with some or all of their money in exchange for bottles of magic elixirs that possessed the power to cure real or imagined ailments. Quacks posing as doctors, German professors, Turks, sorcerers and Indians hawked an endless array of potions to rural Americans. The show would last until every penny had been squeezed from the crowd and the doctor would load his wagon and head down the road to the next gullible audience.

The remedies that were sold by the pitchman were a witch's brew concocted in hotel bathtubs or washtubs. Some were purchased from wholesale manufacturers like The Kickapoo Indian Medicine Company, which was the largest producer of such tonics. Their goodies included: Kickapoo Indian Sagwa, Kickapoo Buffalo Salve, Kickapoo Indian Cough Cure, and Kickapoo Indian Worm Killer. One such remedy promised to "purify the blood, tone up the stomach, quiet the nerves, create an appetite and bring new life into your system." Another promised to "restore lost manhood."

Traveling medicine shows varied greatly in scope. Many traveled by a single horse-drawn wagon and consisted of just two or three black-faced minstrels who sang, played banjo or fiddle, performed skits, and cracked jokes all in an effort to lubricate the pockets of the audience while the "doctor" hawked miracle cures in a bottle.

Larger medicine shows often consisted of as many as forty members who traveled by special trains and carried tents which resembled small circuses. These grand medicine shows often drew crowds by the thousands by offering an exotic mix of jugglers, hypnotists, ventriloquists, snake handlers and trick shooters. Also popular was the Indian medicine show, a small version of Buffalo Bill Cody's Wild West Show. Eventually some shows merged to produce a hodgepodge of buckskin-clad frontiersmen, Indians, German "doctors," Arabian mind-readers, plus an occasional elephant thrown in for good measure.

Despite the dizzying variety of entertainment offered by the medicine shows, music was found to be the most effective means of attracting and holding a crowd. One song called "Wizard Oil" was collected by Carl Sandburg and published in his *American Songbag*.

Wizard Oil

Oh! I love to travel far and near throughout my native land;
I love to sell as I go 'long, and take the cash in hand.
I love to cure all in distress that happen in my way
And you better believe I feel quite fine when folks rush up and say:

    Chorus:
        "I'll take another bottle of Wizard Oil,
          I'll take another bottle or two;
          I'll take another bottle of Wizard Oil,
          I'll take another bottle or two."

HAMLIN'S
WIZARD OIL

THE GREAT MEDICAL WONDER.

There is no Sore it will Not Heal, No Pain it will not Subdue.

HAMLIN'S COUGH BALSAM

PLEASANT TO TAKE
MAGICAL IN ITS EFFECTS.

HAMLIN'S
BLOOD AND LIVER PILLS

For Liver Complaint, Constipation,

AND ALL

Disorders of the Stomach and Digestive Organs.

PREPARED AT THE LABORATORY OI

HAMLINS WIZARD OIL COMPANY, CHICAGO, ILL.

Some medicine shows even encouraged the audience to sing along with the musicians on popular songs of the day. Song books were produced and sold including *Hamlin's Wizard Oil New Book of Songs* and *The Book of Songs As Sung by the Wizard Oil Concert Troupes*.

By the turn of the century, medicine shows were flourishing everywhere. Some worked the big cities, but most stuck to the small town square, vacant lot or county fair. By World War I, medicine shows started to die out at the same time federal and state regulations began to clamp down on quacks and patent medicines. But even into the mid-1940s such prominent old-time musicians as Charlie Monroe, the brother of Bill Monroe, successfully pitched a laxative on his Noonday Jamboree radio program in North Carolina. Charlie even composed a Man-O-Ree theme song to open his shows:

> Man-O-Ree is on the air
> And we hope that you'll be there
> For we want to say hello to one and all,
> If you're feeling down and out, we can say without a doubt,
> What you need right now is Man-O-Ree.

Many Southern musicians who were later to become important to early country music also honed their skills as medicine show musicians. The list would include such luminaries as Uncle Dave Macon, Roy Acuff, Clarence Ashley, Tommy "Snowball" Millard and Gus Cannon.

Bill Monroe.   *Photo courtesy of Bluegrass Unlimited.*

Parlor Music:

The tradition that became known as "parlor music" started with the Civil War. The War brought an outpouring of patriotic and sentimental songs and ballads which celebrated themes important to Americans who were caught in a bitter national struggle. Professional tunesmiths like George W. Root produced songs that tugged at the hearts of the American people and ushered in a new industry based on writing and publishing songs to order. Ballads commemorating a certain battle or event were often composed, printed, distributed and performed within days of the actual event. Within a few years, songsmiths like Charles W. Harris were composing national hits such as "After the Ball" and established the Tin Pan Alley section of New York City as a song-writing headquarters. Harris and others expressed the sentimental mood of a nation with songs of separated sweethearts, aged mothers waiting at home for their wayward sons, hungry orphans, and threadbare newsboys. Sheet music of these and other heart-wrenching themes were sold by the thousands in department and drug stores and even on the street by paper boys. The American public was apparently hungry for such songs and played them on pianos and spinets in the family parlor. Eventually these sentimental songs passed out of public consciousness in big cities when the roaring 'Twenties brought on the Jazz Age. However, these sentimental songs were treasured among rural Southerners and became deeply embedded in their music. An example of this kind of song is "Little Rosewood Casket," found on *Southern Mountain Classics*.

Zeke and Wiley Morris with Ray Atkins, resonator guitar, and Buster Moore, banjo. Knoxville, Tennessee, 1943-1944.

Gospel Music:

If parlor music tugged at the hearts of the American people, then gospel music tugged at its soul. The first gospel or religious music was sung in the earliest days of the American colonies. For those churches without hymnbooks, song leaders would "line out" or "deacon" the psalms and hymns for the congregation to follow in unison. By the 1770s, singing school masters, often traveling by horse or muleback, would stop in a rural Southern community long enough to teach the rudiments of sight reading from the shape-note books then being produced. With the use of different shapes representing the various do rae mi's of the scale, whole congregations were able to learn the basics of harmony singing in short order. Soon harmony singing became common-place in rural churches as shape-note singing became more widespread. Eventually the harmonies learned in church singing began to be used in secular songs. Among the earliest recording artists to feature harmony singing were the Callahan Brothers from Western North Carolina, and the Carter Family, from southwest Virginia.

Carter Family.

How to Read the Tablature

The six lines of the tablature represent the six strings of your guitar. Your first string (the one closest to the floor) will be toward the top of the page and the sixth string will be toward the bottom of the page.

First String

Sixth String

Each number on a line represents the fret on that string that you play. An "O" means you play the string "open" or unfretted.

Third String
Played "open"

Second String
Played at first fret

The rhythm of the tablature corresponds to the rhythm of the music, if you read that stuff. A single stem on a note equals a quarter note. Remember: **Use a down-stroke to play all quarter notes.**

Downstroke

Two notes that are tied together would be eighth notes. Don't forget: **Alternate a down/up stroke with your pick when playing eighth notes: down/up, down/up.**

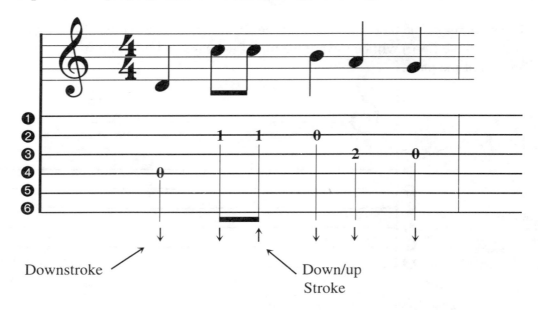

Downstroke

Down/up Stroke

Occasionally, you will find the following symbols in the tablature:

Hammer On: from the fourth string open to the fourth string at the second fret.

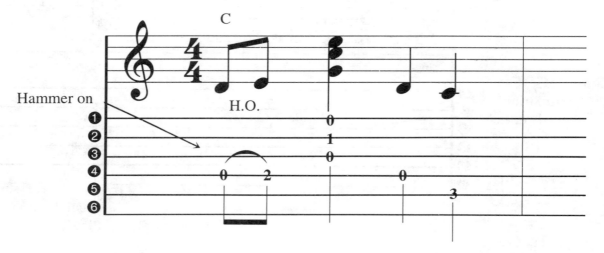

Hammer on

Slide: from the second string at the third fret to the second string at the fifth fret.

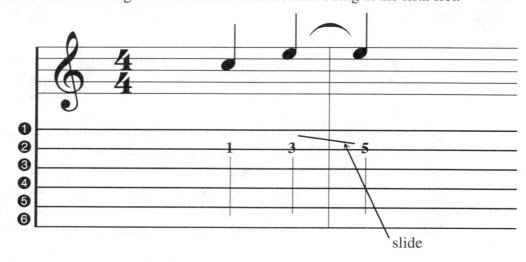

slide

18

Holding the Pick

There are a variety of ways to hold your pick but to get the power to play old-time music, I suggest the following:

1) Start with a tear-drop shaped flatpick of the medium variety.

2) Stick your right hand straight out in front of you at twelve o'clock like you're going to shake howdy to someone. Curve your index finger down to seven o'clock.

3) Balance your pick on the first joint of your index finger with the tip of the pick pointing due West (or nine o'clock).

4) Lower your thumb down on top of the pick to hold it in position.

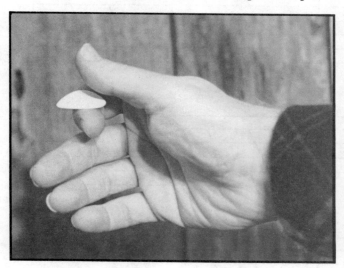 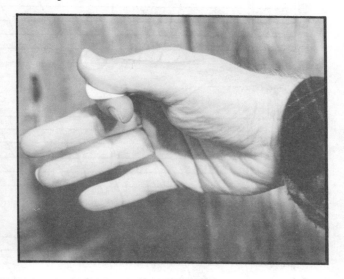

Tips:

1) Keep the fingers of your picking hand open. You can glide your little finger over the pick guard to help you keep track of where you are. Occasionally you may want to plant your little finger firmly on the pick guard kind of like a ball player plants his feet when getting ready to hit a home run.

2) Rest your pick on the sixth string. When hitting the strings, your pick should always be pointed slightly upwards, toward your face.

The Rest Stroke:

The Rest Stroke is what will give you the power and the tone that you crave.

1) Begin by resting your pick on the sixth string. After you hit that string, *follow through* so that your pick lands on the fifth string. If you keep your pick pointed upward, and play that note hard enough, you will *have* to land on the fifth string! As you practice this Rest Stroke, imagine your pick is aiming deep into the bowels of the guitar.

2) Use the Rest Stroke on all quarter notes that you play from here on out.

3) It would be impractical to use the Rest Stroke on eighth notes, because in playing eighth notes, you will be going up/down with your pick.

4) The Rest Stroke is especially effective when playing rhythm guitar, particularly when you want your base strings to be heard.

Chord Structure

Before each tune in the book, there is a section to tell you which chords go where. Each slash mark is a beat. The chord immediately above some slash marks is the actual chord on the tape *Southern Mountain Classics*. This information will come in handy as you line up back-up musicians to accompany you.

Mississippi Sawyer

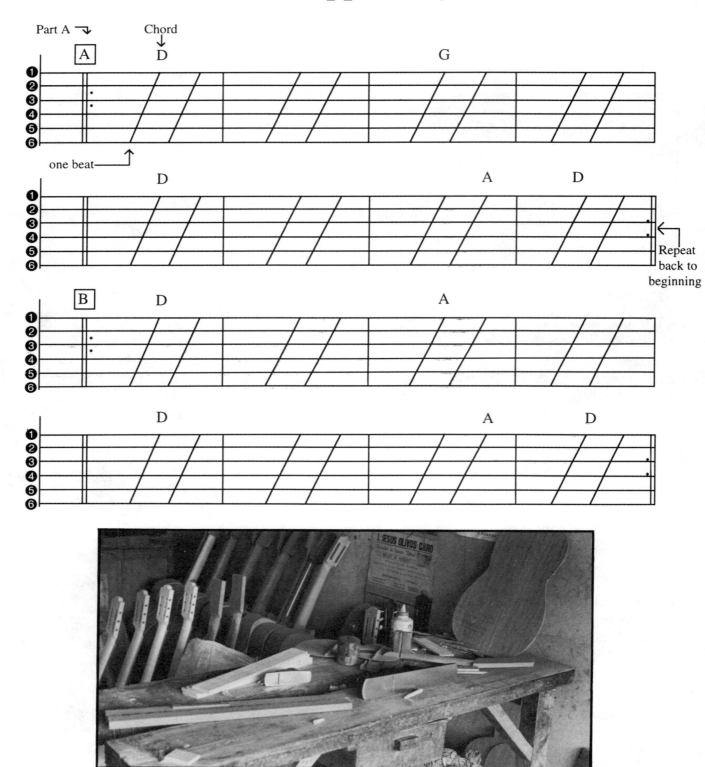

Photo by Wayne Erbsen.

Arkansas Traveler

The tune of "The Arkansas Traveler" was first printed February 23, 1847 and the dialog is generally credited to General Sandford C. Faulkner, who became known as The Arkansas Traveler. Over the years bits of comical lines from other sources have been attached to it.

A squatter was playing his fiddle on the front porch in rural Arkansas when up rides a traveler. The following conversation is said to have taken place:

Traveler: Hello, stranger.

Squatter: Hello yourself.

Traveler: Have you any spirits here?

Squatter: Lots of 'em. Sal seen one last night by that old hollar gum and it nearly skeered her to death.

Traveler: You mistake my meaning. Do you have any liquor?

Squatter: Had some yesterday, but Old Bose he got in and lapped it all out of the pot.

Traveler: You don't understand; I don't mean pot liquor. I'm wet and cold and want some whiskey. Have you got any?

Squatter: Oh, yes—I drunk the last this mornin'.

Traveler: I'm hungry and haven't had a thing since morning. Can't you give me something to eat.

Squatter: Ain't a durn thing in the house. Not a mouthful of meat, nor a dust of meal here.

Traveler: How far is it to the next house?

Squatter: I don't know, I've never been there.

Traveler: As I'm so bold, what might your name be?

Squatter: It might be Dick, and it might be Tom; but it lacks right smart of it.

Traveler: Does this road go to Little Rock?

Squatter: I've lived here 20 years and it ain't gone nowhere yet!

Traveler: Well, how far is it 'till it forks?

Squatter: It don't fork at all; but it splits up like the devil.

Traveler: Does it make any difference which one of these roads I take?

Squatter: Not to me.

Traveler: Is that creek over there fordable?

Squatter: The ducks cross it every day.

Traveler: But how deep's the water?

Squatter: It comes up to "here" on the ducks.

Traveler: Can't you tell me how deep it is?

Squatter: There's water all the way to the bottom.

Traveler: Does the wind blow this-a way all the time?

Squatter: No, sometimes it blows the other way.

Traveler: Your corn's awful little and yellow.

Squatter: We planted the little yellow kind.

Traveler: How'd your taters turn out?

Squatter: They didn't turn out; me and Sal dug them out!

Traveler: I noticed your wife's dress is mighty short.

Squatter: It'll be long enough before she gets another one.

Traveler: How long have you lived here?

Squatter: See that mountain over there? It was here when I arrived.

Traveler: Have you lived here all your life?

Squatter: Not yet.

Traveler: How far did you go in school?

Squatter: About ten miles.

Traveler: No, I mean what grade?

Squatter: Pretty steep.

Traveler: It's raining and I'm not likely to get to another house before dark. Can I sleep here tonight?

Squatter: My house leaks. There's only one dry spot and me and Sal sleeps on it.

Traveler: Why don't you fix the leak?

Squatter: When it's raining I can't, and when it's not, it don't leak.

Traveler: You don't know much.

Squatter: Nope, but I'm not lost.

Traveler: Well, you're not very far from a fool.

Squatter: Just these steps between us.

Traveler: As there seems to be nothing alive about your place but children, how do you do here anyhow?

Squatter: Tolerable well, thank you; how do you do yourself?

Traveler: Why don't you play the balance of that tune?

Squatter: It's got no balance to it.

Traveler: I mean why don't you play the whole of it?

Squatter: Stranger, can you play the fiddle?

Traveler: Yes, a little, sometimes.

Squatter: You don't look like a fiddler but if you think you can play any more of that tune, you can just try it.

The traveler takes the fiddle and plays the whole of it.

Squatter: Stranger, take half a dozen chairs and sit down! Sal, stir yourself round like a six-horse team in a mud hole and cook this gentleman and me some supper. And while you're at it, raise up the board under the head of the bed and bring out the black jug of whiskey. We've got visitors!

Photo by Margaret Morley.
Courtesy of North Carolina Division of Archives and History.

Arkansas Traveler

Key on *Southern Mountain Classics:* D

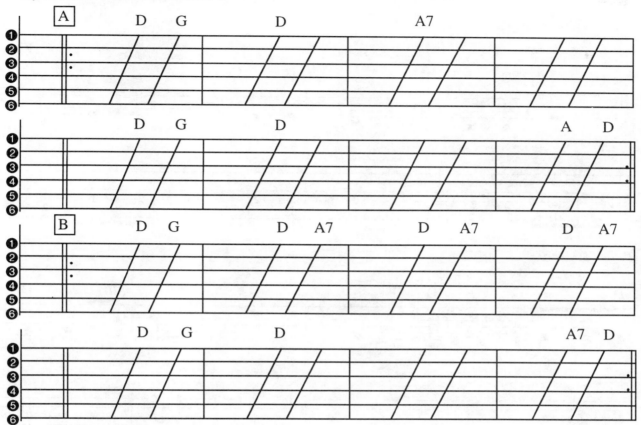

Note: Each slash mark represents one beat.

Photo reproduced from the collections of the Library of Congress.

ARKANSAS TRAVELER

Version I

ARKANSAS TRAVELER

Version II

Key of D

Chicken Reel

Even without words, there is a certain humor to "Chicken Reel." It almost has its own rhythm, like the strut of a triumphant chicken just after laying an egg. It was a favorite of Carl Sandburg who wrote, "The trickiest of all is Chicken Reel. Cunning of musical design, elusive and unexpected in its transitions, it is like a poem that parodies itself, like a cat that walks alone, like a woman who forgets that she has forgotten, like three thistle sifters with thimbles sifting softly through the sieves."

"Chicken Reel" was first printed on June 25, 1910 and claimed by Joseph M. Daly of Boston.

Key on *Southern Mountain Classics:* D

CHICKEN REEL

Key of D

CHICKEN REEL

Version II

Key of D

27

Cluck Old Hen

While modern country singers seem to like to sing about pick-up trucks, trains, mother and jail, old-time musicians often found the chicken to be a worthy subject of numerous songs. ("Cacklin' Hen," "Chicken Reel," "Rise When the Rooster Crows," "Cacklin' Pullet," "Who's That Knockin' on the Henhouse Door," "Cacklin' Hen and Rooster Too," "Chicken Don't Roost Too High For Me" and "C-H-I-C-K-E-N").

Key on *Southern Mountain Classics:* A Minor

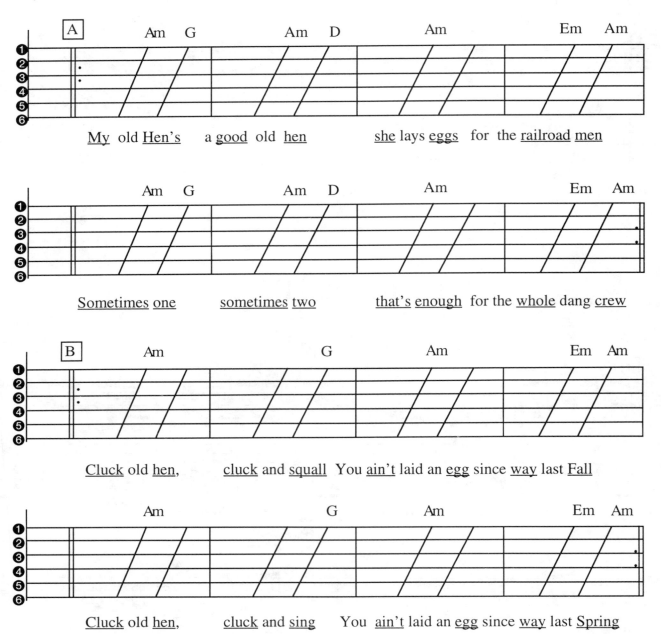

My old Hen's a good old hen she lays eggs for the railroad men

Sometimes one sometimes two that's enough for the whole dang crew

Cluck old hen, cluck and squall You ain't laid an egg since way last Fall

Cluck old hen, cluck and sing You ain't laid an egg since way last Spring

CLUCK OLD HEN

Version I

Photo by Wayne Erbsen.

CLUCK OLD HEN

Key of A Minor

Version II

My old hen's a good old hen,
She lays eggs for the railroad men
Sometimes one, sometimes two
Sometimes enough for the whole dang crew

    Cluck old hen, cluck and squall
    You ain't laid an egg since 'way last Fall
    Cluck old hen, cluck and sing
    You ain't laid an egg since 'way last Spring

My old hen, she won't do
She lays eggs and taters too
First time she cackled, she cackled in the lot
Next time she cackled, she cackled in the pot

I had a little hen, she had a wooden leg
Best darn hen that ever laid an egg
Laid more eggs than any hen around the barn
Another little drink wouldn't do me any harm

Cluck old hen, cluck and tell you
If you don't cluck, I'm gonna sell you
The old hen cackled, she cackled for corn
The old hen cackled when the chicken's all gone

My old hen's a good old hen
She lays eggs for the railroad men
Sometimes eight, sometimes ten
That's enough for the railroad men

The old hen cackled, she cackled for corn
The old hen cackled when the chicken's all gone
That old hen's she's raised on a farm
Now she's in new ground digging up corn

Fisher's Hornpipe

"Fisher's Hornpipe" is the most popular hornpipe played in America, closely followed by "Ricketts Hornpipe" and "Durang's Hornpipe." These later hornpipes, by the way, were named after John Bill Ricketts and John Durang, who were dancers that toured America with professional dance troupes.

The term "hornpipe" originally was meant to describe a primitive European wind instrument that was also called the pibgorn or a stockhorn. It was apparently made out of the shin bone of a sheep, with a cow horn attached as a bell.

"Hornpipe" was also a term used to describe a dance which originally used the instrument of the same name for accompaniment. The dance was popular in both America and England between 1770 and 1850 and featured fancy footwork. The dance later became associated with sailors, who performed it with folded arms.

Hornpipes were usually played at a slower pace than reels. This was probably done to accommodate the intricate steps of those dancing the hornpipe. It was also due to the fact that the tunes themselves were often quite intricate. With the decline in popularity of the hornpipe as a dance, musical hornpipes began to be played at faster speeds until they were virtually identical to reels. The faster speeds, however, often meant that many of the subtleties of the tunes were lost.

"Fisher's Hornpipe" first appeared in print in London around 1780 in "Sixteen Cotillions, Sixteen Minuets, Twelve Allemands and Twelve Hornpipes Composed by J. Fischar" where it was entitled simply "Hornpipe I." James A. Fischar was the musical director at the Covent Garden in London. By 1800, the other tunes in Fischar's book were apparently forgotten, but "Hornpipe I" was widely popular under the title "Fisher's Hornpipe."

Photo reproduced from the collections of the Library of Congress.

Fisher's Hornpipe

Key on *Southern Mountain Classics:* D

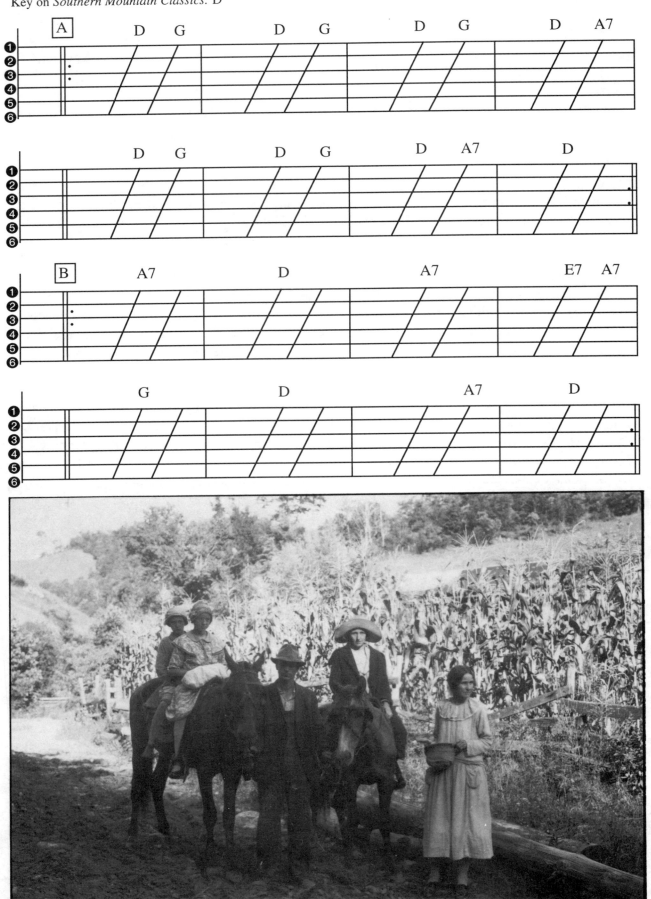

Photo by Edward M. Ball, Southern Highlands Research Collection, Asheville, North Carolina.

FISHER'S HORNPIPE

Version I

Key of D

FISHER'S HORNPIPE

Version II

Key of D

Hogeye

"Hogeye" has led a checkered life. It was born as a sea shanty between 1849-50 during the gold rush in California. In the mad scramble to get to the gold fields, many would-be prospectors made their journey to California aboard sailing ships which rounded the Horn and docked at the port of San Francisco. Once docked, barges carried men and goods to their destinations. These barges were known as "hog-eyes." After it was composed, "The Hog-Eyed Man" headed out to sea and was collected in the far away English towns of Newcastle and Lancashire. Occasionally it masqueraded under the title "Row the Boat Ashore." Landlubbing versions of "The Hog-Eyed Man" were reported in Wisconsin, South Carolina, Kentucky, Alabama, and North Carolina. These versions completely shed all connection with its seagoing past. All that remains is the sand in Sally's garden.

This version of "Hogeye" actually bears more resemblance to two other tunes, "Sally in the Garden" and "Fire on the Mountain" than it does to the sea shanty known as "The Hog-Eyed Man." In structure it shares a similar first part with "Fire on the Mountain," except that "Hogeye" is set to a modal scale. I must confess I changed the tune and chords slightly by replacing the "one" chord at the end of the first line with a "four" chord. The tag on the end of the tune bears the trademark of "Fire on the Mountain," and gives the tune a crooked lilt. As if this wasn't quite confusing enough, the verses were borrowed from even more songs. The "Chicken in the bread pan" verse has been caught strutting from song to song and even shows up in some versions of tunes like "Soldier's Joy." The business about asking Sally if her dog bites and blaming her poor daddy for cutting the dog's biter off, was borrowed from the tune "Granny Will Your Dog Bite."

The source of this version of "Hogeye" can be traced to its earliest recording in February, 1928 by Pope's Arkansas Mountaineers. The group was organized by J.D. Pope and his son, Milton Pope, who ran a piano store in Searcy, Arkansas. Strangely, neither played on any of the band's eight recordings.

Remember, the verses are only sung to the first part. Don't try playing this tune for a proper contra or square dance. Its crooked melody and zany chords will make the caller go prematurely bald.

Note: The last measure leads you to the beginning. When you are ready to end, simply omit the last two notes in the last measure and hold the note before that, which is the third string at the second fret (A), for two beats.

Photo by Edward M. Ball,
Southern Highlands Research Collection,
Asheville, North Carolina.

Hogeye

Key on *Southern Mountain Classics:* A

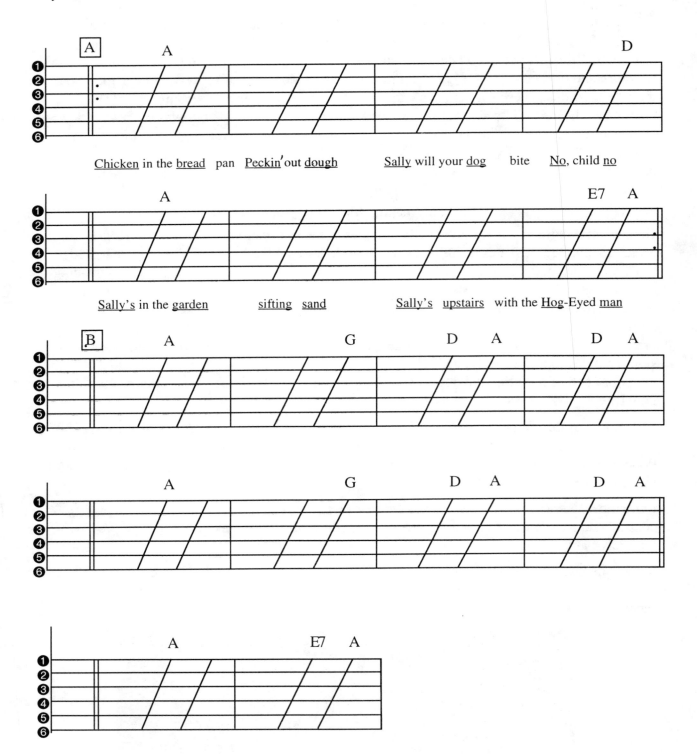

Chicken in the <u>bread</u> pan <u>Peckin'</u> out <u>dough</u>   <u>Sally</u> will your <u>dog</u>   bite   <u>No</u>, child <u>no</u>

<u>Sally's</u> in the <u>garden</u>   <u>sifting</u> <u>sand</u>   <u>Sally's</u> <u>upstairs</u> with the <u>Hog</u>-Eyed <u>man</u>

HOGEYE

Version I

Key of A

HOGEYE

Version II

Chicken in the bread pan
Peckin' out dough
Sally will your dog bite
No, child no

Sally's in the garden.
Sifting sand.
Sally's upstairs
With the Hog-Eyed Man

Sally's in the garden
Sifting, sifting.
Sally's upstairs
With the Hog-Eyed Man

Sally will your dog bite
No, child no.
Daddy cut his biter off
A long time ago

Photo reproduced from the collections of the Library of Congress.

John Henry

John Henry, known as the steel driving man, ranks right up there with our finest mythical characters such as Paul Bunyon, Santa Claus and the Tooth Fairy. It is the classic American ballad that pits man against machine. The ballad is supposedly based on an actual contest between John Henry and a steam-powered drill held at the Big Bend tunnel in West Virginia about 1870-72. John Henry beat the steam drill fair and square, but his valiant efforts cost him his life.

This unusual version of "John Henry" comes from the playing of Fred Cockerham and others from the Round Peak area of North Carolina. Since they didn't usually sing many of the verses, included are the words sung by Fiddlin' John Carson. Fiddlin' John recorded it as "John Henry Blues" and waxed it for OKeh in late March 1924, making it the earliest recording of the song.

When you are singing along with this arrangement of "John Henry," keep in mind that the last two lines of the verses are repeated. You can either sing the last two lines again, or you can simply sing them the first time and just play it instrumentally the second.

Photo reproduced from the collections of the Library of Congress.

John Henry

Key on *Southern Mountain Classics:* A

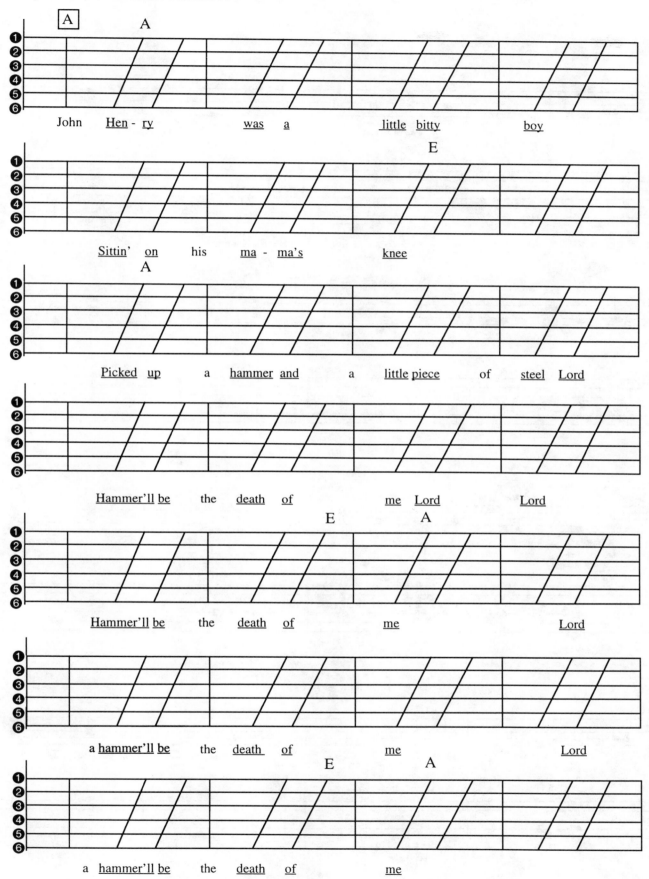

John   Hen - ry   was   a   little bitty   boy

Sittin' on   his   ma - ma's   knee

Picked up   a   hammer and   a   little piece   of   steel Lord

Hammer'll be   the   death of   me Lord   Lord

Hammer'll be   the   death of   me   Lord

a hammer'll be   the   death of   me   Lord

a hammer'll be   the   death of   me

JOHN HENRY

Version I

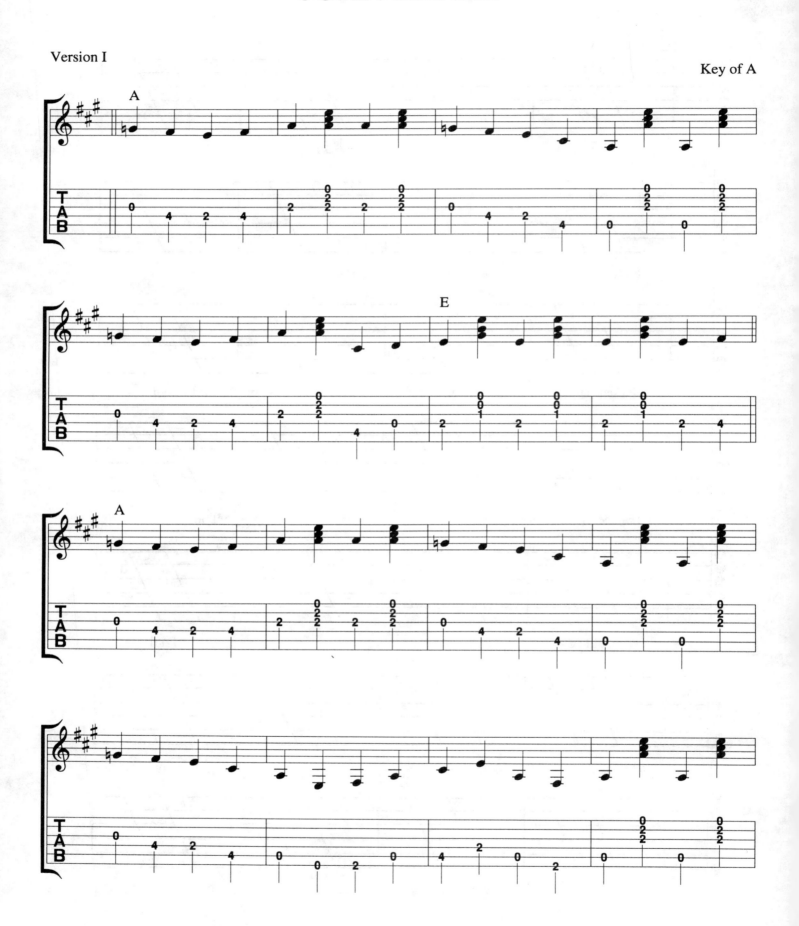

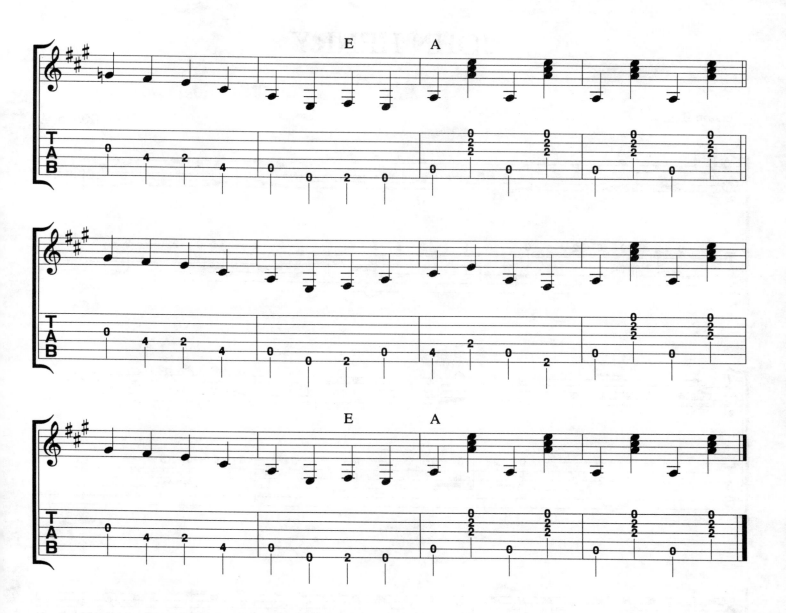

Riley Puckett.

JOHN HENRY

Version II

Key of A

John Henry was a little bitty boy
Sittin' on his mama's knee
Picked up a hammer and a little piece of steel
"Lord, a hammer'll be the death of me
Lord, a hammer'll be the death of me"

John Henry went upon the mountain
Come down on the other side
The mountain was so tall, John Henry was so small
Lord, he lay down his hammer and he cried, "Oh, Lord"
He lay down his hammer and he cried

John Henry was on the right hand
But that steam drill was on the left
"Before your steam drill beats me down
I'll hammer my fool self to death
Lord, I'll hammer my fool self to death"

John Henry told his Captain
"Captain, you go to town,
Bring me back a twelve-pound hammer
And I'll whup your steam drill down
And I'll whup your steam drill down"

For the man that invented that steam drill
Thought he was might fine
John Henry drove fourteen feet
The steam drill only made nine
The steam drill only made nine

John Henry told his shaker
"Shaker, you better pray
For if I miss this six-foot steel
Tomorrow'll be your buryin' day
Tomorrow'll be your buryin' day"

John Henry told his little woman
"I'm sick and I want to go to bed
Fix me a place to lie down
Got a rollin' in my head
Got a rollin' in my head"

John Henry had a lovely little woman
Her name was Polly Ann
John Henry got sick and he had to go to bed
But Polly drove steel like a man
Polly drove steel like a man

47

Leather Britches

"**L**eather Britches" is an old tune that may have descended from the Irish air entitled "The Britches On" which was collected in Petrie's *The Complete Collection of Irish Music* (1902). Petrie believes it is related to a well-known Scottish reel entitled "McDonald's" which was sometimes known as "Lord McDonald's." What is known for sure is that "Leather Britches" was a popular tune both before and during the Civil War. It is still a fiddler's favorite perhaps because it is just tricky enough to make it interesting. It's almost like there is an unspoken rule that says learning to play it means unofficial acceptance into the ranks of old-time musicians. Jack Link, of the Gipsy Gippos, once told me that if you can play "Leather Britches," you can play "anything." The tune is usually played as an instrumental dance tune but once in a while someone will holler out the first verse. Verses two and three are rather rare and were collected by Frank C. Brown from Miss Pearle Webb in Pineola, Avery County, North Carolina in 1922. Verse four was collected in Kentucky by Jean Thomas and published in *Devil's Ditties*. The last verse comes from Breene County, Pennsylvania, compliments of Samuel P. Bayard.

Bayard also contributes an interesting notion about "Leather Britches" in his *Hill Country Tunes*. Bayard speculated that "Leather Britches" seemed related to the well-known plantation song "Shortenin' Bread." This notion at first seemed perposterous until I simplified "Leather Britches" down and found a remarkable similarity between the two melodies.

Key on *Southern Mountain Classics:* G

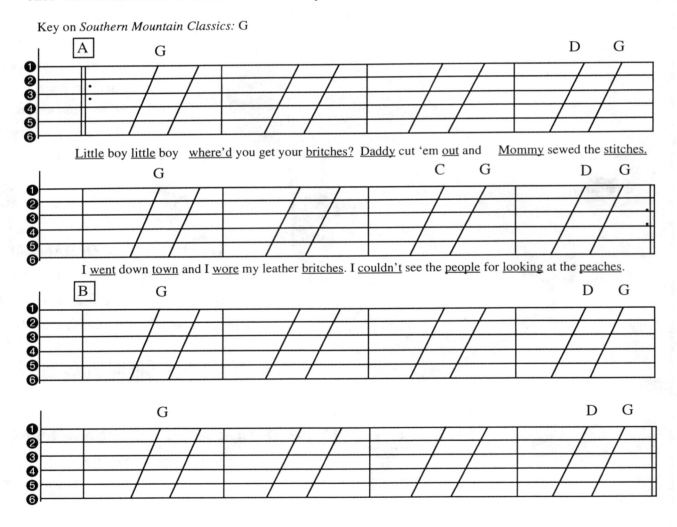

Little boy little boy where'd you get your britches? Daddy cut 'em out and Mommy sewed the stitches.

I went down town and I wore my leather britches. I couldn't see the people for looking at the peaches.

LEATHER BRITCHES

Version I

Key of G

Photo reproduced from the collections of the Library of Congress.

LEATHER BRITCHES

Version II

Key of G

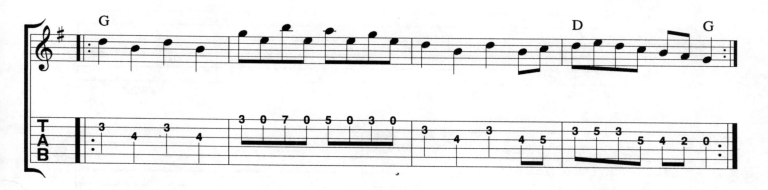

Little Boy, Little boy
Where'd you get your britches?
Daddy cut 'em out
And Mommy sewed the stitches.

I went down town
And I wore my leather britches.
I couldn't see the people
For looking at the peaches.

I went down town
And I got a pound of butter.
I came home drunk
And I throwed it in the gutter.

Leather britches, finger stitches,
Mammy sewed the stitches in.
Pappy kicked me out of bed,
I had my leather britches on.

Leather britches full of stitches,
Old shoes and stockings on.
My wife she kicked me out of bed
Because I had my britches on.

Little Rosewood Casket

The beautiful, simple melody and plaintive words of "Little Rosewood Casket" make it a classic old-time tune. Entitled "A Package of Old Love Letters," it was composed in 1870 by Louis P. Goullard and C.A. White.

Key on *Southern Mountain Classics:* C

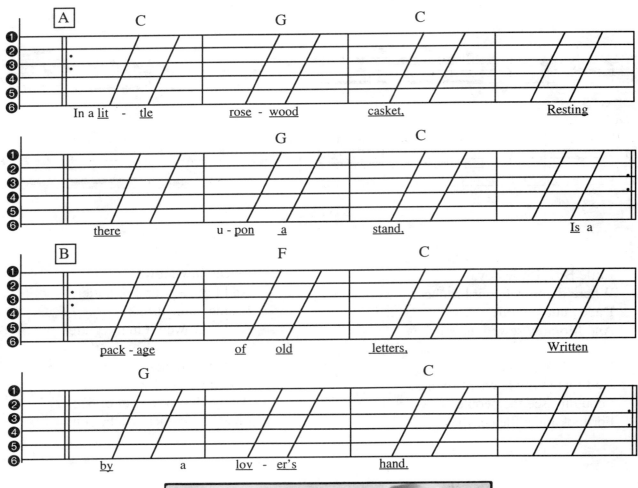

A C   G   C

In a lit - tle   rose - wood   casket,   Resting

G   C

there   u - pon   a   stand,   Is a

B   F   C

pack - age   of   old   letters,   Written

G   C

by   a   lov - er's   hand.

The Delmore Brothers.

54

LITTLE ROSEWOOD CASKET

Version I

Key of C

LITTLE ROSEWOOD CASKET

Version II

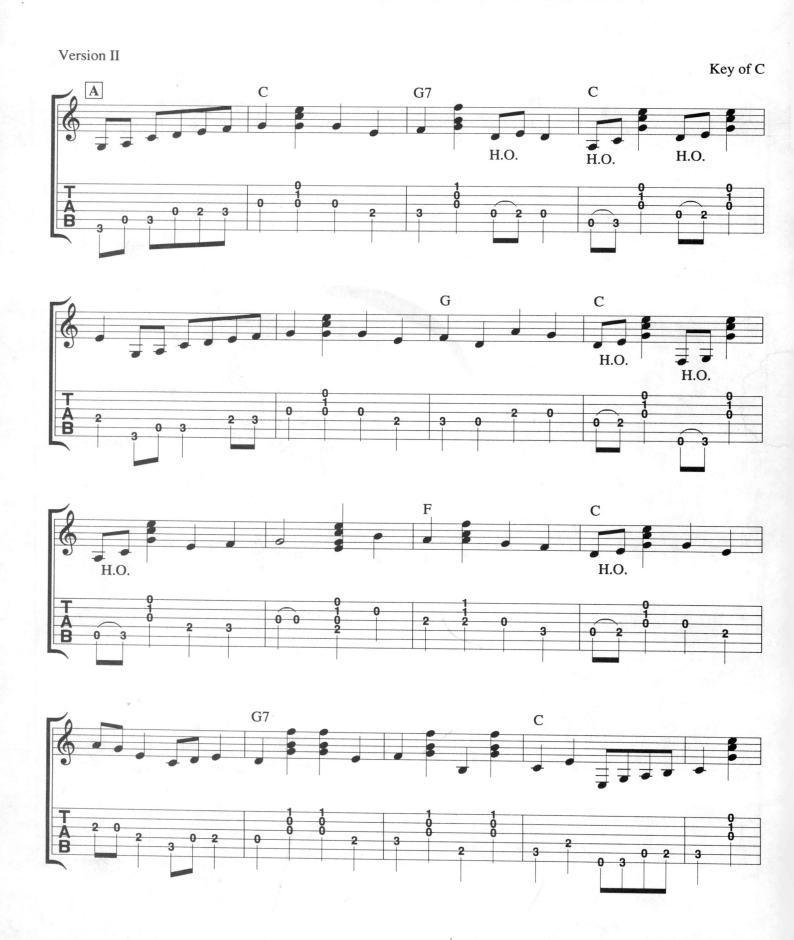

In a little rosewood casket,
Resting there upon a stand
Is a package of old letters
Written by a lover's hand.

You may go and bring them, sister
Sit down here upon my bed
And take gently to your bosom
My poor aching, throbbing head.

You have brought them, thank you sister.
You may read them o'er me.
I have often tried to read them
But for tears I could not see.

When I'm resting in my coffin
And my shroud around me's wound
And my narrow bed is ready
In the pleasant churchyard ground.

Take this package of old love letters
Strew them all around my heart.
But this little ring he gave me
From my finger never part.

I must say farewell, dear sister,
Place my hands upon my breast.
I am dying, kiss me sister,
I am going home to rest.

Carl Sauceman.

Mississippi Sawyer

Even to this day, "Mississippi Sawyer" has maintained its reputation as being among the most popular fiddle pieces of all time. Most people have assumed the tune originated in the state of Mississippi. However, Ira W. Ford wrote in his 1940 book, *Traditional Music of America,* that the tune came from an early day sawmill owner who became known as "The Mississippi Sawyer." According to this story, the miller set up one of the earliest sawmills in the West near the junction of the Ohio and Mississippi rivers. The mill became quite a local attraction among early pioneers whose only means of producing building lumber had been with a broadaxe, maul, and wedge.

This story tells that on the day the mill was to open, a huge celebration took place that lasted for days. People came in covered wagons, horseback, and on foot. The first logs that were fed into the mill were turned into a dance platform and picnic tables for the ensuing feast. When the millwright admitted to being a fiddler, he was chosen to play the opening tune of the dance. The tune he chose to christen the mill with has since been known as "Mississippi Sawyer." Research has shown that "Mississippi Sawyer" is based on an earlier tune known as "The Downfall of Paris." The main difference between these two tunes is that "Mississippi Sawyer" contains just two parts, while "The Downfall of Paris" has four. If the story about the millwright is true, perhaps he played "The Downfall of Paris," thus giving it a new name.

However, Samuel P. Bayard wrote in his *Dance to the Fiddle, March to the Fife* that he suspected the word "Sawyer" actually referred to a tree trunk or stump that stuck up in the Mississippi River, endangering navigators. He collected one interesting version of the tune that merged the first part of "Tennessee Wagoner" with the second part of "Mississippi Sawyer." The resulting tune was called "Mississippi Wagoner."

It seems that the only fact about "Mississippi Sawyer" you can depend on is that it is always played in the key of D.

Zeke and Wiley Morris at Radio WWNC, 1946.

Mississippi Sawyer

Key on *Southern Mountain Classics:* D

Sheep Herders, 1900.   *Photo credit: Jim Bollman Collection.*

MISSISSIPPI SAWYER

Version I

MISSISSIPPI SAWYER

Version II

Key of D

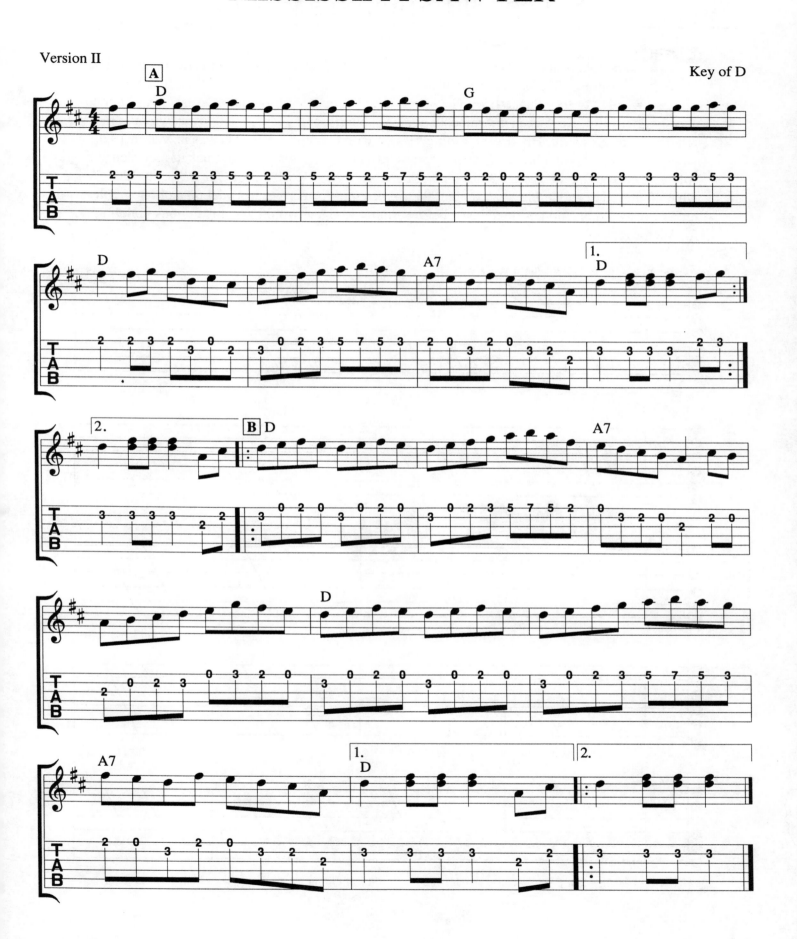

The Old Spinning Wheel

"The Old Spinning Wheel" was recorded by Riley Puckett and Ted Hawkins in San Antonio, Texas on March 30, 1934 and released on Bluebird (B5432), and Montgomery Ward (M-498). Puckett, who had been called "The Bald Mountain Caruso" was blinded shortly after birth. He was an enormously popular guitarist and vocalist with over two hundred recordings to his credit. His first recording session with Columbia Records was in March 1924 when he recorded with chicken farmer/fiddler Gid Tanner. At this session, Puckett recorded six solo numbers with guitar and vocals. One of the vocals was "Rock All of Our Babies to Sleep" which featured his yodeling, making him the first country performer to yodel on a phonograph record. It would be another three years before Jimmy Rodgers would wax his famous yodeling for Victor Records.

Key on *Southern Mountain Classics:* D

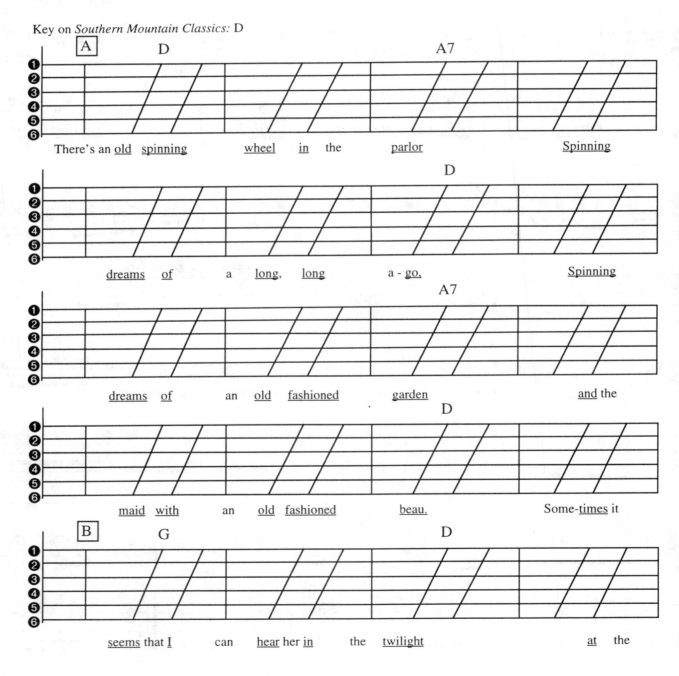

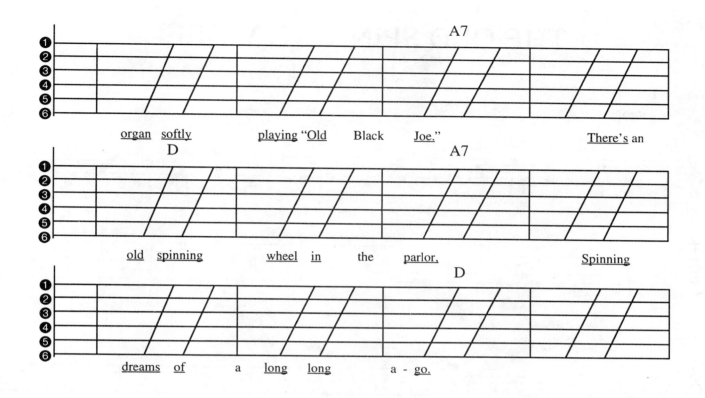

A7

organ softly   playing "Old   Black   Joe."   There's an

D   A7

old spinning   wheel   in   the   parlor,   Spinning

D

dreams of   a   long   long   a - go.

Photo credit: William A. Barnhill Collection, Pack Memorial Library, Asheville, North Carolina.

THE OLD SPINNING WHEEL

Version I
Capo 2

Key of C

THE OLD SPINNING WHEEL

Version II
Capo 2

Key of C

67

There's an old spinning wheel in the parlor
Spinning dreams of a long, long ago
Spinning dreams of an old fashioned garden
And the maid with an old fashioned beau.

Sometimes it seems that I can hear her in the twilight
At the organ softly singing "Old Black Joe"
There's an old spinning wheel in the parlor
Spinning dreams of a long, long ago.

Photo by Gideon T. Laney.
Courtesy of David C. Anderson.

Red Rocking Chair

T he haunting tune known as "Red Rocking Chair" is also played and sung with slight variations under such titles as "Rain and Snow," "Red Apple Juice," and "Sugar Babe Blues." Among this group, only "Rain and Snow" has a second part, which I borrowed for this version of "Red Rocking Chair."

Key on *Southern Mountain Classics:* A Minor

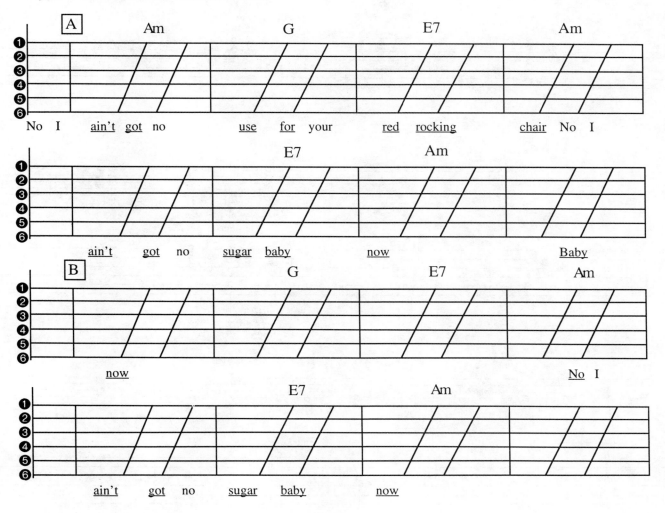

RED ROCKING CHAIR

Version I

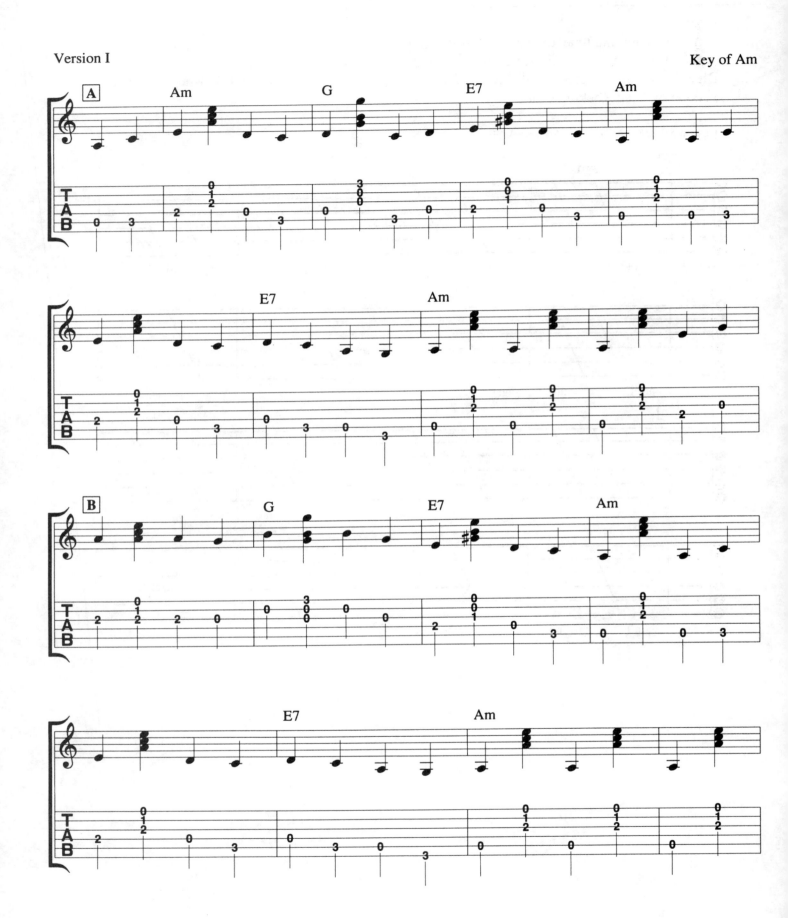

RED ROCKING CHAIR

Version II

No I ain't got no use
For my red rocking chair.
No I ain't got no sugar baby now,
Baby now.
No I ain't got no sugar baby now.

Some old rounder come along
Took my sugar babe and gone,
And I ain't got no sugar baby now,
Baby now.
No I ain't got no sugar baby now.

I gave her every cent I made
And I laid her in the shade,
And I ain't got no sugar baby now,
Baby now.
No I ain't got no sugar baby now.

And it's who'll call you honey
And it's who'll sing this song?
And it's who'll rock the cradle when I'm gone?
When I'm gone?
And it's who'll rock the cradle when I'm gone?

Oh I ain't got no use
For your red apple juice.
I'm living on your corn squeezings now,
Squeezings now.
Yes I'm living on your corn squeezings now.

Red Parkam. *Photo by Bob Linsey, courtesy Asheville Chamber of Commerce.*

Shady Grove

"**S**hady Grove" is a favorite song of the mountains. Also called "Little Betty Ann," it is composed mainly of verses that "float" from song to song. Since the tune is known to have only one part, I composed the second part for the recording on *Southern Mountain Classics*.

Key on *Southern Mountain Classics:* A Minor

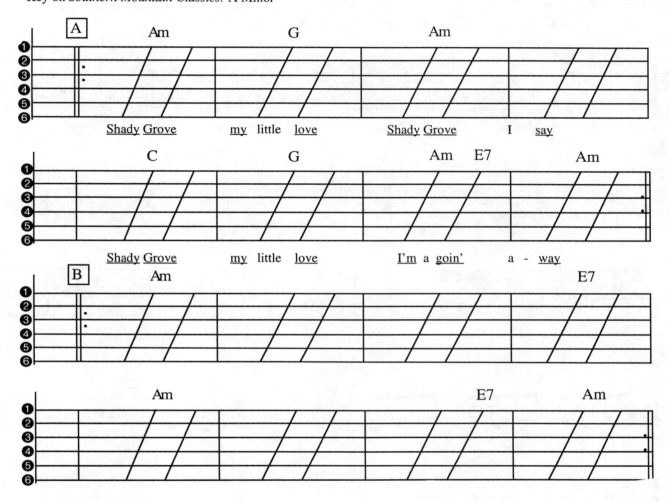

David C. Anderson on Guitar.
Photo by Gideon T. Laney.

SHADY GROVE

Version I

Key of A Minor

SHADY GROVE

Version II

Key of A Minor

Shady Grove, my little love,
Shady Grove I say.
Shady Grove my little love
I'm a goin' away.

I went to see my Shady Grove
Standing in the door.
Shoes and stockings in her hands,
Little bare feet on the floor.

Wished I had a big fat horse
Corn to feed him on.
Shady Grove to stay at home
Feed him while I'm gone.

Peaches in the summertime,
Apples in the fall.
If I can't get the girl I love
I won't have none at all.

Lips as red as a blooming rose,
Eyes the deepest brown.
You are the darling of my heart,
Stay 'til the sun goes down.

Sixteen horses in my team,
The leader he is blind.
Ever I travel this road again,
There'll be trouble on my mind.

If I had a needle and thread
As fine as I could sew,
I'd sew that pretty girl to my side
And down the road I'll go.

Fifteen miles of mountain road,
Twenty miles of sand.
If I ever travel this road again
I'll be a married man.

Lester Flatt.

76

Soldier's Joy

"**S**oldier's Joy" must be the most well known of all fiddle tunes. A favorite of Southern soldiers during the Civil War, it was often called "Payday in the Army," "Love Somebody" and "Sweet Sixteen." Some say it's a descendant of an 18th century English tune called "The King's Head." The story goes that a condemned man attempted to save himself by playing this tune for the king.

The first known recording of "Soldier's Joy" was by the Skillet Lickers in Atlanta, Georgia on October 29, 1929. Included on the recording were Gid Tanner and Clayton McMichen on fiddles, Riley Puckett on guitar and Fate Norris on banjo.

Here are the words that Clayton McMichen used to introduce the tune:
"Well, folks, here we are again, The Skillet Lickers, red hot and rarin' to go. We're going to play you another little tune this morning. I want you to grab that gal, shake her foot and moan. Don't you let 'em dance on your new carpet. You make 'em roll it up."

Key on *Southern Mountain Classics:* D

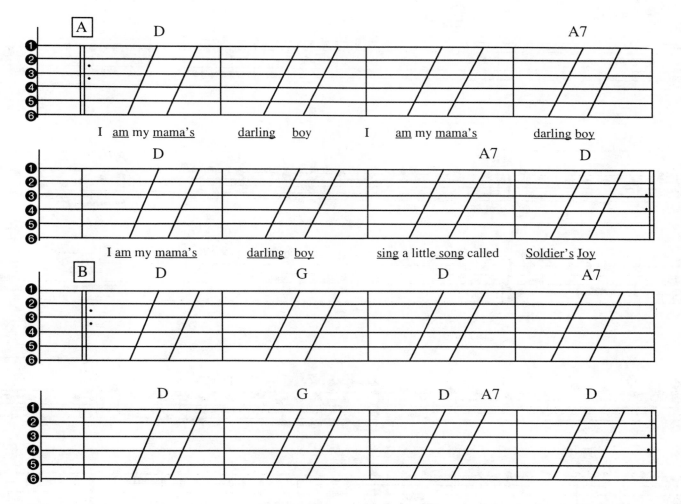

77

SOLDIER'S JOY

Version I

SOLDIER'S JOY

Chicken in the bread pan scratching out dough
Grannie will your dog bite, no child no.
Ladies to the center and gents catch air
Hold her there don't let her rare.

Grasshopper sitting on a sweet potato vine
Grasshopper sitting on a sweet potato vine
Grasshopper sitting on a sweet potato vine
Along come a chicken and says, "You're mine!"

I'm gonna get a drink, don't you want to go
I'm gonna get a drink, don't you want to go
I'm gonna get a drink, don't you want to go
All on Soldier's Joy.

Twenty-five cents for the morphine
Fifteen cents for the beer.
Twenty-five cents for the morphine
They're gonna take me away from here.

I am my mama's darling boy
I am my mama's darling boy
I am my mama's darling boy.
Sing a little song called "Soldier's Joy."

I love somebody, yes I do
I love somebody, yes I do
I love somebody, yes I do,
And I bet you five dollars, you can't guess who.

I'll be sixteen in '92
I'll be sixteen in '92
I'll be sixteen in '92.
I love somebody but I won't say who.

Riley Puckett.
Photo courtesy of John Edwards Memorial Foundation.

The State of Arkansas

"The State of Arkansas" has been sung under such titles as "The Arkansas Traveler," "The Arkansas Navy," "The Arkansas Emigrant," "Bill Stafford" and "When I Left Arkansas." It tells a harrowing saga of Stamford Barnes who started out his misadventure in St. Louis and traveled on by train to Arkansas where he landed in a fleabag hotel. The verses will tell you the rest of the story.

Ancestors of "The State of Arkansas" have been traced to a nineteenth century English sea chanty, "Canada I O," which, in turn, is thought to have descended from the 18th century Scots love song, "Caledonia."

Notwithstanding its illustrious history, three Americans claimed to have composed it. This version probably originated in the 1880s. The earliest known version was hand written by in the George Williams in Bollinger County, Missouri in 1906 with the note, "This the boys out in the country like to sing. I heard it several years ago by a man named Lincoln. He had no education; he was a hired man." In the text we have preserved the original spelling of "Arkansaw."

Key on *Southern Mountain Classics:* A Minor

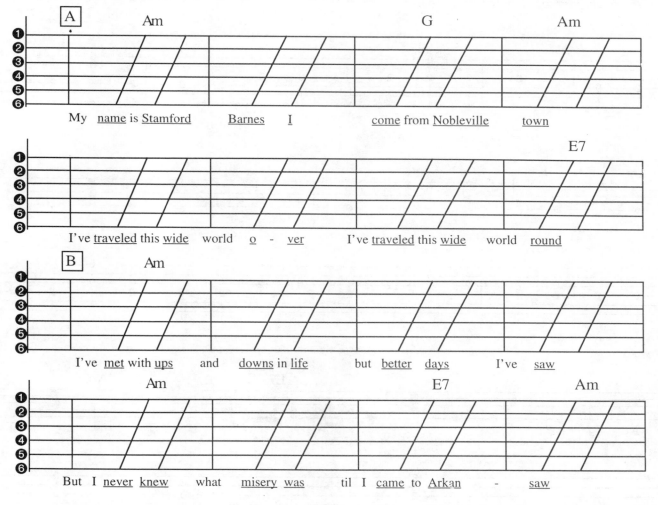

81

STATE OF ARKANSAS

Version I

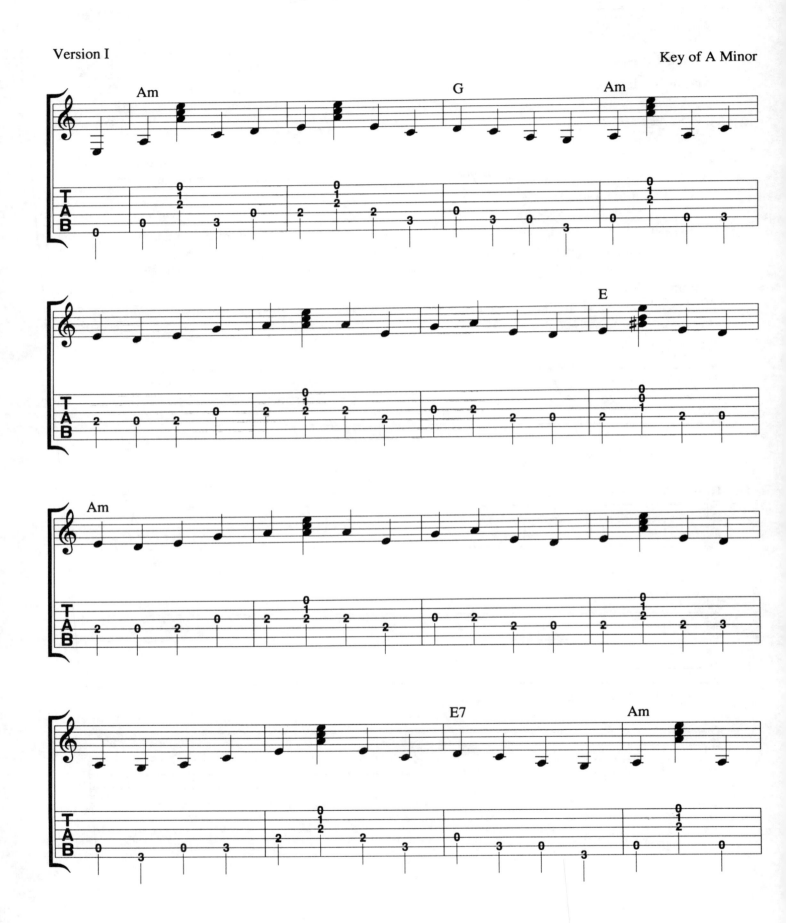

STATE OF ARKANSAS

Version II

My name is Stamford Barnes, I come from Nobleville town;
I've travelled this wide world over, I've traveled this wide world round.
I've met with ups and downs in life but better days I've saw,
But I never knew what misery was until I came to Arkansaw.

I landed in St. Louis with ten dollars and no more;
I read the daily papers till both my eyes were sore;
I read them evening papers until at last I saw
Ten thousand men were wanted in the state of Arkansaw.

I wiped my eyes with great surprise when I read this grateful news,
And straightaway off I started to see the agent, Bill Hughes.
He says pay me five dollars and a ticket to you I'll draw
It'll land you safe upon the railroad in the state of Arkansaw."

I started off one evening a quarter after five;
I started from St. Louis, half dead and half alive;
I bought me a quart of whiskey my misery to thaw,
I got drunk as a biled owl when I left for old Arkansaw.

I landed in Ft. Smith one sultry Sunday afternoon,
It was in the month of May, the early month of June,
Up stepped a walking skeleton with a long and lantern jaw,
Invited me to his hotel, "The best in Arkansaw."

I followed my conductor into his dwelling place;
Poverty were depictured in his melancholy face.
His bread it was corn dodger, his beef I could not chaw;
This was the kind of hash they fed me in the state of Arkansaw.

I started off next morning to catch the morning train,
He says to me, "You'd better work, for I have some land to drain.
I'll pay you fifty cents a day, your board, washing, and all,
You'll find yourself a different man when you leave old Arkansaw."

I worked six weeks for the son of a gun, Jesse Herring was his name,
He was six foot seven in his stocking feet and taller than any crane;
His hair hung down in strings over his long and lantern jaw,
He was a photograph of all the gents who lived in Arkansaw.

He fed me on corn dodgers as hard as any rock,
Until my teeth began to loosen and my knees began to knock;
I got so thin on sassafras tea I could hide behind a straw,
And indeed I was a different man when I left old Arkansaw.

Farewell to swamp angels, cane brakes, and chills;
Farewell to sage and sassafras and corn dodger pills.
If I ever see this land again, I'll give to you my paw;
It will be through a telescope from here to Arkansaw.

Uncle Joe

"Uncle Joe" started out its long life as a Scottish tune that became known as "Miss McCleod's Reel." The first known printing of the tune was in 1809 in Niel Gow's book entitled *A Collection of Strathspey Reels* published in Edinburgh under the title "Mrs. McCleod of Raasay's Reel." This version contained the note, "An original Isle of Sky Reel. Communicated by Mr. McCleod."

What a surprise to find out that our "Miss" McCleod had a Mr. McCleod! The tune apparently made the perilous journey to America aboard a crowded ship and became a favorite of fiddlers playing for dances. By 1856 it was spotted in Putnam County, Georgia, and was published in Joel Chandler Harris' *Uncle Remus*. The tune of "Miss McCleod's Reel" has stubbornly resisted change, but the words have often been improvised, and are known under such titles as "Uncle Joe," "Did You Ever See The Devil Uncle Joe?," "Hop High Ladies," "Old Mammy Knicker-bocker," "Don't You Want to Go to Heaven," "The Virginia Reel" and "John Brown." It is often played in the key of G.

Note about the Chords: The version of "Uncle Joe" recorded on *Southern Mountain Classics* is a bit unusual in that it goes to a D7 chord at the end of the second, fourth, sixth, and eighth lines. Commonly, the tune will go to a G in those places. You can play it either way and be in good company.

Key on Southern Mountain Classics: G

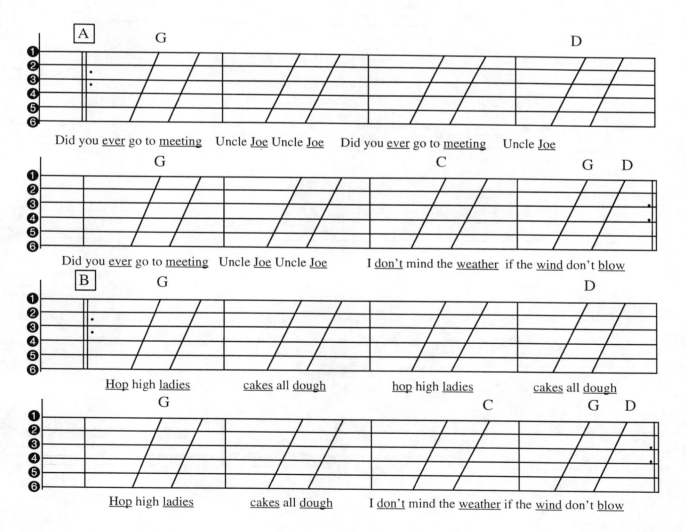

UNCLE JOE

Version I   Key of G

UNCLE JOE

Version II

Did you ever go to meeting Uncle Joe, Uncle Joe?
Did you ever go to meeting Uncle Joe?
Did you ever go to meeting Uncle Joe, Uncle Joe?
I don't mind the weather if the wind don't blow.

Hop high ladies, cakes all dough
Hop high ladies, cakes all dough
Hop high ladies, cakes all dough
I don't mind the weather if the wind don't blow.

Will your horse carry double Uncle Joe, Uncle Joe?
Will your horse carry double Uncle Joe?
Will your horse carry double Uncle Joe, Uncle Joe?
I don't mind the weather if the wind don't blow.

How's your rheumatism Uncle Joe, Uncle Joe?
How's your rheumatism Uncle Joe? .
How's your rheumatism Uncle Joe, Uncle Joe?
I don't mind the weather if the wind don't blow.

Is your horse a single footer, Uncle Joe, Uncle Joe?
Is your horse a single footer, Uncle Joe?
Is your horse a single footer, Uncle Joe, Uncle Joe?
I don't mind the weather if the wind don't blow.

Don't you want to go to heaven, Uncle Joe, Uncle Joe?
Don't you want to go to heaven by and by?
Don't you want to go to heaven, Uncle Joe, Uncle Joe?
Where the 'possum and the sweet potatoes grow up in the sky?

How do you like the ladies, Uncle Joe, Uncle Joe?
How do you like the ladies, Uncle Joe?
How do you like the ladies, Uncle Joe, Uncle Joe?
I don't mind the weather if the wind don't blow.

Harvey and Leonard Copeland.
Photo courtesy of John Edwards Memorial Foundation.

J.P. Fisher.

Photo by Bob Lindsey, courtesy of Asheville Chamber of Commerce.

When You and I Were Young, Maggie

Lest we forget, "Maggie" was written as a poem by Canadian George W. Johnson, who was a scholar and poet. He wrote the poem about his student and sweetheart Maggie Clark, and about the old mill where they used to meet. Johnson published the poem himself in a collection named *Maple Leaves*. The poem caught the eye of the English composer/conductor James Austin Butterfield who set the tune to it while living in Chicago. The real Maggie and George Johnson were married in 1865, but alas, she died that same year before knowing that the song about her would be published the following year and become a classic.

Key on *Southern Mountain Classics:* D

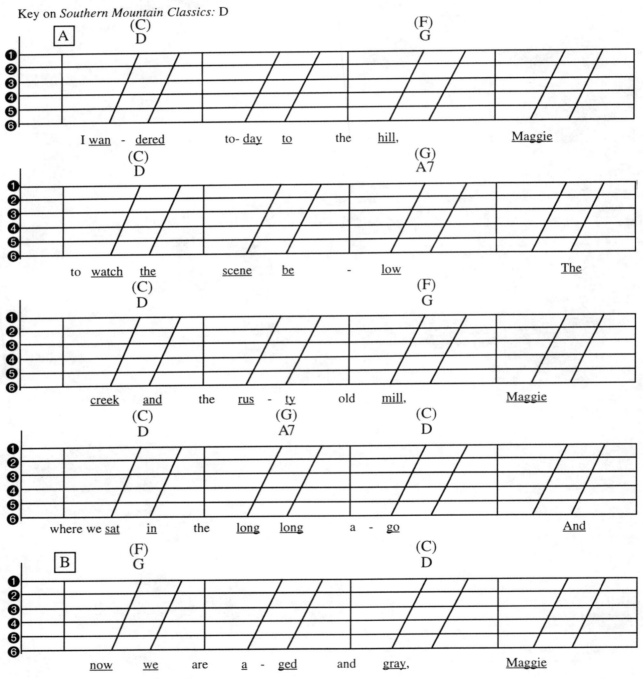

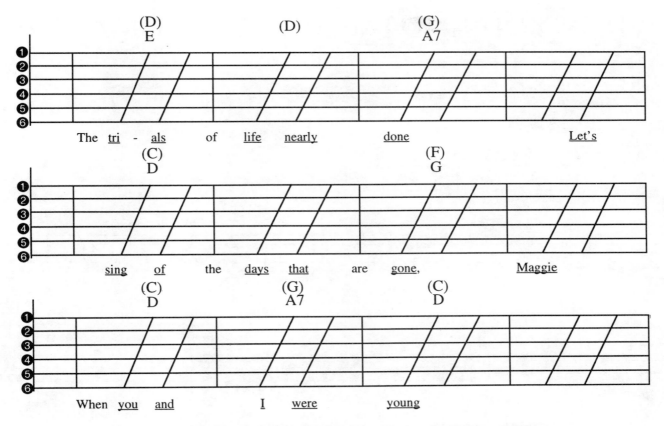

	(D)		(D)		(G)		
	E				A7		

The tri - als of life nearly done Let's

	(C)			(F)			
	D			G			

sing of the days that are gone, Maggie

	(C)		(G)		(C)		
	D		A7		D		

When you and I were young

Blue-Ridge Hillbillies.

91

WHEN YOU AND I WERE YOUNG, MAGGIE

Version I
Capo 2

Key of C

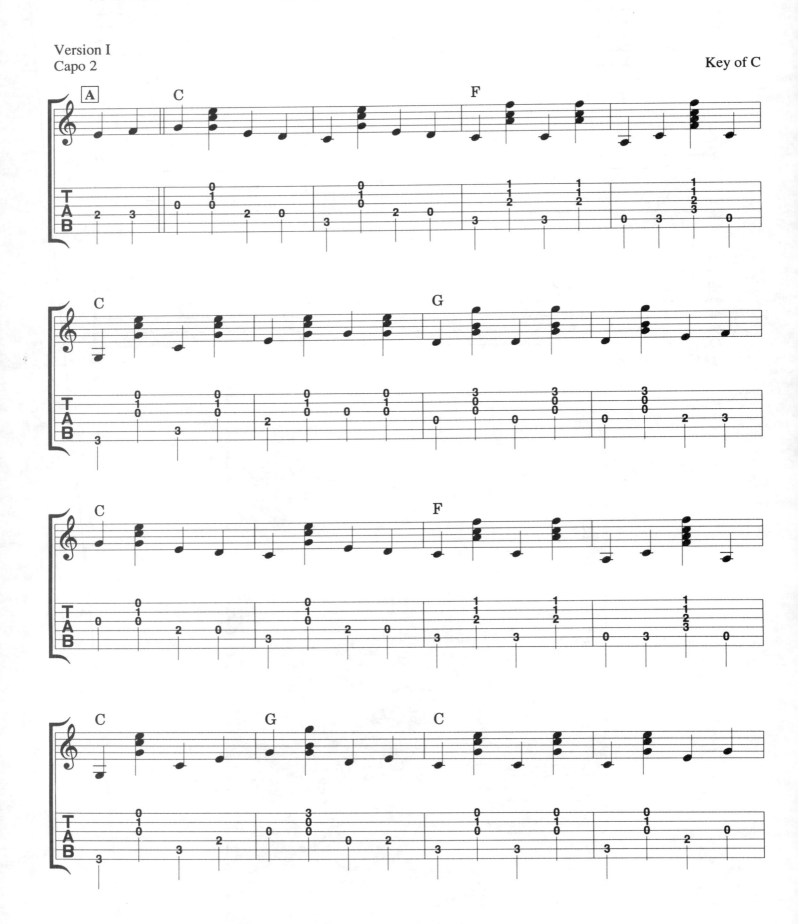

WHEN YOU AND I WERE YOUNG, MAGGIE

Version II
Capo 2

Key of C

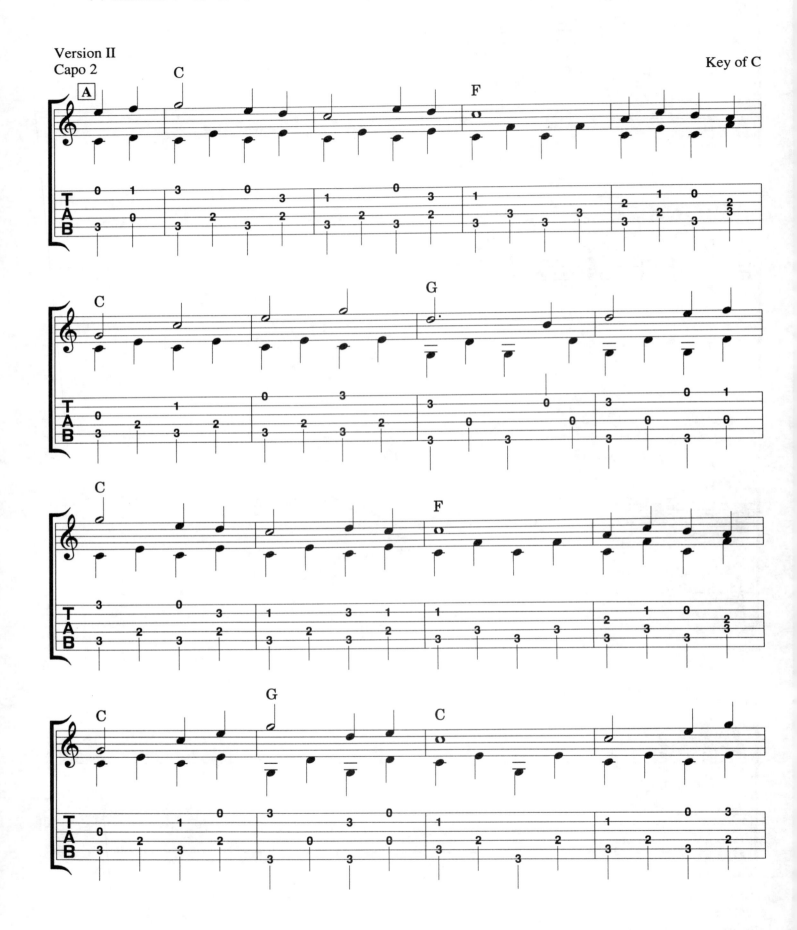

WHEN YOU AND I WERE YOUNG, MAGGIE

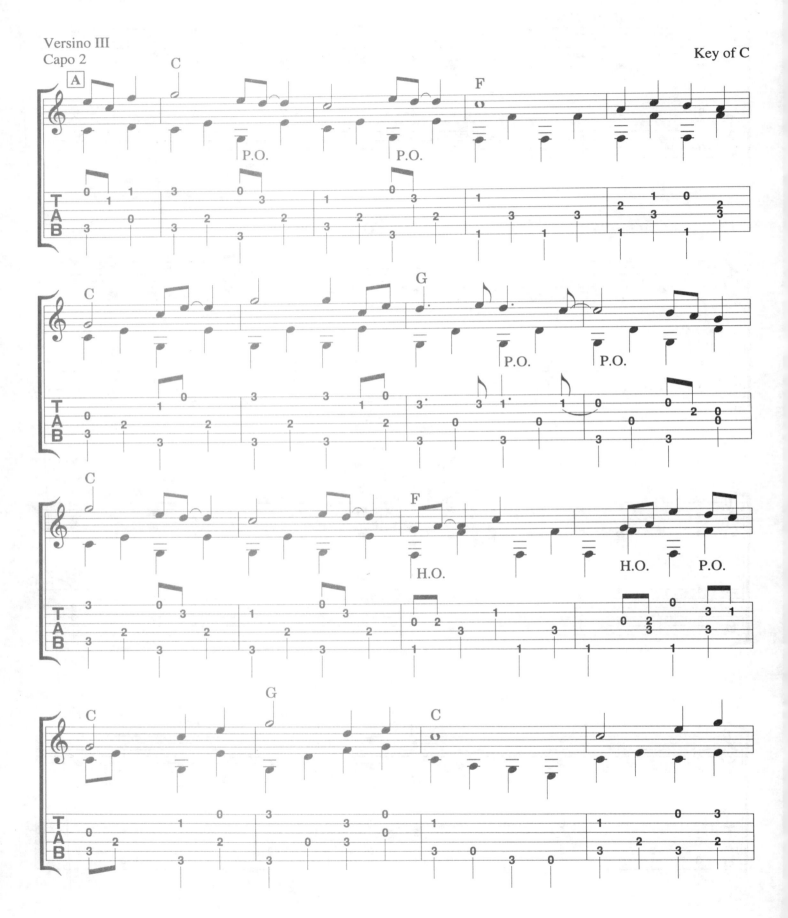

I wandered today to the hill, Maggie
To watch the scene below
The creek and the old rusty mill, Maggie
Where we sat in the long long ago

Green grove is gone from the hill, Maggie
Where first the daisies had sprung
The old rusty mill is now still, Maggie
Since you and I were young

And now we are aged and gray, Maggie,
The trails of life nearly done
Let's sing of the days that are gone, Maggie
When you and I were young

A city so silent and lone, Maggie
Where the young and gay and best
In polished white mansions of stone, Maggie
Where they each found a place for their rest

Is built where the birds used to play
And join in songs that were sung
We sang just as gay as did they, Maggie
When you and I were young

They say I am feeble with age, Maggie
My steps less sprightly than then
My face is a well-written page, Maggie
Then but time, time alone was the pen

They say we are aged and gray, Maggie
As spray from white breakers flung
To me you're as fair as you were, Maggie
When you and I were young

Southern Mountain Classics

*S*outhern Mountain Guitar grew out of the recording entitled *Southern Mountain Classics.* When we recorded it on May 21st and June 6th of 1991, we had no idea just how many people would enjoy the music nor did we envision that this series of instruction books would grow out of it. I knew the music was infectious, but I didn't know just how much!

In recording *Southern Mountain Classics,* what we had in mind was simply to capture a good music session among friends. It was recorded at National Public Radio station WCQS in Asheville, North Carolina where I've hosted a traditional music radio show called *Country Roots* for the past twelve years. With the gracious help of Dick Kohl as engineer, we simply played the tunes we knew best. There was no overdubbing and few "re-takes."

The music we chose to record included some of the classics of old-time mountain music. Some are square dance fiddle tunes like "Soldier's Joy," "Mississippi Sawyer," "Uncle Joe," "Leather Britches" and "Arkansas Traveler." Other tunes such as "Shady Grove," "The State of Arkansas," "Red Rocking Chair" and "Hogeye" represent the lonesome and scarce sounds of mountain music. For good measure we threw in some clogging feet, an instrumental version of the ballad of "John Henry," and several sentimental old parlor tunes like "Little Rosewood Casket" and "The Spinning Wheel."

The performers who recorded *Southern Mountain Classics* are the same high-caliber musicians who have kept old-time music alive down through the years. Dirk Powell, whose family hails from Kentucky, has more than established himself as a first-rate fiddler. John Herrmann is an ace clawhammer banjo player with the reputation of being the father of old-time music in Japan. Meredith McIntosh is a solid bass player who is equally at home on the fiddle or guitar. Don Pedi is a master on the mountain dulcimer and Phil Jamison is a well-respected dance caller and a full-fledged member of Ralph Blizzard's New Southern Ramblers.

Henry Whitter.
Photo courtesy of John Edwards Memorial Foundation.

Guitar Chords

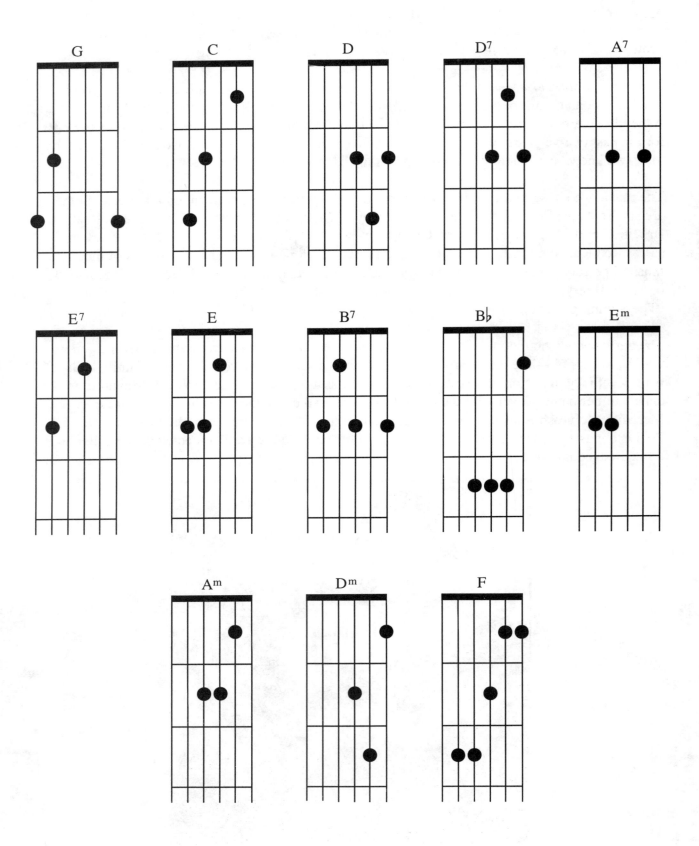

Thanks!

Southern Mountain Guitar grew out of the recording *Southern Mountain Classics.* Both, in away, were the result of jam sessions. The musicians jammed when they recorded it, and those who contributed to this book jammed when they gave their time, hard work, ideas and energy. Thanks to my wife, Barbara Swell, and Janet Swell Webb of PageScape Publications for editing, Steve Millard for cover design, Bill Bay for conceiving of this book series and to all the friends and musicians who have lent their talents to this project: Dirk Powell, John Herrmann, Don Pedi, Phil Jamison, Meredith McIntosh, Dick Kohl, Bob Willoughby, Ray Alden, Wayne W. Daniel, Bucky Hanks, Joan Moser, Robert Winans, Neal Hellman, Mike Seeger and Lori Erbsen.

J.E. Mainer and the Crazy Mountaineers.
Photo courtesy of Bluegrass Unlimited.

Books & Recordings by Wayne Erbsen

Instruction Books

Clawhammer Banjo For the Complete Ignoramus!
Bluegrass Banjo Simplified!!
Starting Bluegrass Banjo From Scratch
Painless Mandolin Melodies
The Complete & Painless Guide to the Guitar
Southern Mountain Banjo
Southern Mountain Fiddle
Southern Mountain Mandolin
Southern Mountain Guitar
Southern Mountain Dulcimer

Songbooks

The Backpocket Old-Time Songbook
The Backpocket Bluegrass Songbook
The Front Porch Old-Time Songbook
The Old-Time Gospel Songbook
Cowboy Songs, Jokes, Lingo 'n Lore
Crawdads, Doodlebugs & Creasy Greens

Recordings

Native Ground
Old-Time Gospel Instrumentals
Old-Time Gospel Favorites
Southern Mountain Classics
Southern Soldier Boy
The Home Front
Ballads & Songs of the Civil War
Cold Frosty Morning
Front Porch Favorites
Cowboy Songs of the Wild Frontier
Raccoon and a Possum

To Order, Contact:
Native Ground Music
109 Bell Road
Asheville, N.C. 28805
(704) 299-7031 or (800) 752-2656

About the Author

Wayne Erbsen has been actively involved in old-time music for the past thirty years as a musician, author, teacher, recording artist, publisher and radio host. He has written fourteen instruction books and songbooks and has recorded fifteen albums. For the past eleven years he has worked as the Director of the Appalachian Music Program at Warren Wilson College in Asheville, North Carolina where he makes his home with his wife Barbara and their three children, Wes, Rita and Leann. Wayne also runs his own publishing/recording company business, Native Ground Music.

Wayne Erbsen.   *Photo by Bucky Hanks.*